ELVIS
UNCENSORED ON THE RECORD

BY ANTHONY MASSALLY

INTERVIEWS CONDUCTED BY GARY MOORE

CODA
BOOKS LTD

C⊕DA
BOOKS LTD

www.codabooks.com

This edition is published in Great Britain in 2012 by

Coda Books Ltd., Office Suite 2, Shrieves Walk, 39 Sheep Street, Stratford-upon-Avon, Warwickshire CV37 6GJ

www.codabooks.com

Copyright © 2012 by Coda Books Ltd.

All rights reserved. No part of this publication may be reproduced or transmitted in any form or by any means, electronic or mechanical, including photocopy, recording, or any information storage and retrieval system, without permission in writing from the publisher.

Interviews © Archive Media Publishing Ltd.

Photographs courtesy of Pictorial Press, Empics, The Library of Congress and The National Archives and Records Administration.

A CIP catalogue record for this book is available from the British Library.

ISBN: 978-1-78158-251-0

CONTENTS

THE KING REMEMBERED 4

TRACK-BY-TRACK ANALYSIS 74

DJ FONTANA IN HIS OWN WORDS
INTERVIEW CONDUCTED BY GARY MOORE 119

SCOTTY MOORE IN HIS OWN WORDS
INTERVIEW CONDUCTED BY GARY MOORE 135

ABOUT CODA BOOKS 154

THE KING REMEMBERED

It's impossible to overstate the influence of Elvis Presley, the impact his life and work had on popular music, or the size of the Presley industry that has snowballed globally since his death almost three decades ago. A host of musicians from the Beatles to Cliff Richard and beyond were first inspired to pick up a guitar in anger by Elvis' early records, and a whole new film genre – lightweight musical drama – was fostered by a whole series of films in which he acted, to an equal mixture of hysteria and derision.

Elvis Aaron Presley was born on January 8, 1935 and died at the age of only 42 on August 16, 1977. His career went through several distinct phases, beginning with the raw rock'n'roll he performed on 1950s records released by the Sun label in Memphis, Tennessee, which most critics regard as his finest work. At this stage his influences were gospel, country and hillbilly music, which he fused with elements borrowed from black rhythm and blues to create a whole new sound. In the following decade he was rapidly eclipsed by the wave of rock and pop music that transformed the world and threatened to make him obsolete, especially as he was spending most of his time in films. However, in the 1970s he returned to a kind of stadium-level respectability, even if his music was less astonishing than before and his credibility was undermined by health issues caused by drug dependency and weight gain. All the stages of his career have attracted millions of fans, making him the most successful solo singer in history, rivalled only by Frank Sinatra, who was helped by the fact that his active career was twice as long as Presley's.

One of the key elements of the Elvis myth is his rise to superstardom from a background in extreme poverty. His father, Vernon (a truck driver) and mother Gladys (a sewing machine operator) lived in East Tupelo, Mississippi, and were rocked by a series of catastrophes in Elvis' early life, starting with the stillbirth of his twin, who was named Jesse Garon. When Elvis was only three years old, Vernon served eight months for forgery in the notorious Parchman Penitentiary, during which time Gladys lost the family home and the Presleys lived with their in-laws. Events such as this, and the evident poverty that plagued the family, made Elvis something of a loner after he started school at the age of six. His closest relationship was with his mother, and would remain so until her death in 1958, when Elvis was 23.

In 1945 Elvis entered and came second in a contest at the Mississippi-Alabama Fair and Dairy Show, where he sang Red Foley's 'Old Shep', winning $5. The following year he was given a guitar as a present and was taught to play it by his uncle and a local pastor.

At school Elvis began to absorb the blues and country music of America's Deep South – and in particular Memphis, where the Presleys moved in 1948 – and by his early teens he had begun to effect an image which reflected his outsider status. Growing sideburns and sporting a ducktail and quiff (which led to minor blows with authority, such as the school football coach), Elvis spent much time listening to music in Memphis' black quarter and in particular Beale Street, where blues and R&B were the standard fare.

As Elvis told a press conference in Las Vegas in 1969, "When I was a boy, I always saw myself as a hero in comic books and in movies. I grew up believing this dream... When I got outta high school I was driving a truck. You know, I was just a poor boy from Memphis... I was driving a truck and training

to be an electrician. I suppose I got wired the wrong way round somewhere along the line!"

Elvis' school friend and later bodyguard Red West told Todd Slaughter, president of the UK fan club: "[At school] we had crew cuts, wore T-shirts and blue jeans. Elvis had the long ducktail, the long sideburns and he wore the loud clothes and naturally he was a target for all the bullies, and one day luckily I walked into the boys' bathroom at Humes High School and three guys were going to cut his hair just, you know, to make themselves look big or make them feel big or whatever, and I intervened and stopped it, and I guess that stuck, because a couple of years later, after Elvis had his first record, he came over and asked me if I would like to go with him – I think it was Grenada, Mississippi or somewhere – and I went, and I was with him from then on, except for a couple of years in the Marine Corps."

In 1953 Elvis graduated from school and worked as a machinist and truck driver. At around the same time, the Sun record-label owner Sam Phillips was credited with saying that he was looking for "a white man with a negro sound and the negro feel" – because he thought that black music such as blues would be popular among the white population if the right white artist could be found to sing it. Coincidentally, Elvis recorded two demo acetates at Sun studios in July that year, the first of which was a present for his mother. The songs were all popular ballads of the day and of little interest, but Phillips and assistant Marion Keisker liked the discs and asked Elvis to play with local musicians Scotty Moore and Bill Black. During a break after jamming on some standards on July 5, 1954, the band slipped into an impromptu rendition of Arthur Crudup's 'That's All Right Mama', which Phillips heard and thought might add a new flavour to the music of the day. He duly released the song as a single and watched in shock as it went stratospheric…

Elvis recounted this story at a Las Vegas press conference: "One day, I went into a recording studio and made a record for a guy named Sam Phillips on Sun Records. He put the record out in about a week. I went back to driving a truck and just forgot about it. Man, that record came out and was real big in Memphis. They started playing it, and it got real big. Don't know why. The lyrics had no meaning. I was just this kid, who went awopah-awh-a-awh on record… Anyway, they put the record out and it got pretty big in the South. But I still had my job. I was driving a truck daytimes and working nightclubs at night… and things like that."

Scotty Moore, Elvis' guitarist, remained a celebrated figure all his life, telling Music City Recorders in 1973 of the song's origins: "Sam and I would meet every day, drinking coffee and kicking around ideas where music was going and what we should look for. In our conversations he mentioned that a young fellow had been in some time prior to cut a record for his mother. And he said he had impressed him very much and they had kept his name on file and I said, 'Would you get him in and audition?' So for a period of three or four weeks, every day that I saw Sam I asked him had he contacted the guy, and he said no he hadn't. Finally he gave me Elvis's name and his telephone number and said, 'Why don't you call him, have him come up to your house and just have him sing a few things for you and see what you think, and then we set up an audition here in the studio?' So I said fine, so that night – I think it was on a Saturday I believe – I called Elvis, told him who I was, who I was working with and could he come over the next day, which was Sunday. He said he could."

Moore went on: "So Elvis came over… he had all the pink shirt, pink pants with the typical ducktail hairstyle at the time, white shoes… he was a little ahead of his time for the way he was dressed, which didn't bother me one way or the other, because

I was interested in what he sounded like singing. We sat around for a couple of hours and he sang several different songs. At that time, Bill Black lived just a few doors down from me on the same street, and he came over and listened for a while, and Elvis left and I asked Bill, 'Well, what do you think?' He said, 'Well, he sings good. He didn't really knock me out, you know'. I said, 'Well, that's my opinion, too,' I said, 'but if we got the right song and recorded it the right way...' So I called Sam and told him basically the same thing – the boy sings fine, and in my opinion it would only be a matter of finding the right song and as to what direction, how he was recorded."

Moore recalled the songs that Elvis had come up with: "He sang some Marty Robbins songs, some Hank Snow songs, some Roy Hamilton, some of the current R&B hits at the time... a little bit of everything really. So then Sam did call him and set a time for us to go into the studio the following night. It was just me and Bill [as] a background, just to give us an idea of how he would sound like on tape. We went in and went through several different songs and nothing was really happening, because you know it was an audition, and then we were taking a break, sitting around drinking coffee. Elvis started clowning around, he picked up his guitar and started dancing around and started singing 'That's All Right Mama', and Bill picked up his bass, started slapping it, just more or less clowning and I joined in and that's it... really it's just one of those things. Well, the rest, of course, is history. The audition turned into the actual first session and out of that came 'That's All Right Mama'."

Elvis' later friend and co-singer Charlie Hodge said: "Elvis liked all kinds of music. He had a lot of albums... various artists in the country, pop and gospel field. He would often listen to Mario Lanza. Even in Memphis as a young man, Elvis would go to a place called Blues Alley and spend hours listening to blues singers. He would listen to gospel and even symphony music. He could appreciate all kinds of different and varied musical styles; he just adored gospel, JD Sumner & The Stamps Quartet… JD would often let Elvis in the back door whenever the Blackwood Brothers were singing. In those days Elvis was so poor he couldn't afford to pay to see the group perform, so JD let him in. Elvis never forgot what JD did for him."

Once Elvis hit the big time, his life was suddenly thrown upside down. As he explained at the Canada press conference in 1957, life on the road could be stressful: "Well, uh, take for instance last night. We had a show in Vancouver. I didn't sleep any until about 10 o'clock today. I just get all keyed up, and it's tough to relax… touring is the roughest part. It's really rough. Because, I mean, you're in a town and you do a show, you come off, you ride in a car, you go to the next town [and] I have to prepare for a show that night. And therefore I have to rest – and we have rehearsals in the afternoon. So I don't have much time. I'm actually pressed for time. It's not that I'm trying to avoid [the fans], because that's certainly not it. It's just that I'm rushed for time and I have to make every moment count when I'm on the road."

The influence of Elvis' new sound on the musicians of the day was profound and immediate. As country star Waylon Jennings later wrote, "'What if' – I asked my dad one day in the early 1950s – 'they mixed black music with white music? Country music and blues?' 'That might be something', Daddy replied. On a fall morning in 1954, listening to KVOW's Hillbilly Hit Parade, I heard that something. I was taking my brother to school. It was about 8.20, and the reason I remember is that the programme was only on for 15 minutes each day, from 8.15 to 8.30 am. Elvis was singing 'That's All Right Mama' and 'Blue Moon of Kentucky'. The sound went straight up your spine. The way he sang, the singer sounded black. Maybe it was the flapping of the big doghouse bass, all wood thump, and the slapback echo of the guitars wailin' and frailin' away. It just climbed right through you. I had grown up hearing Bill Monroe sing 'Blue Moon of Kentucky', but this was something entirely different. I thought, what a wild, strange sound…"

None other than Johnny Cash recalled in his book Cash – The Autobiography: "There were a lot of white people listening to 'race music' behind closed doors. Of course, some of them (some of us) were quite open about it, most famously Elvis.

Elvis was already making noise in Memphis when I got there in 1954. Sam Phillips had released his first single, 'That's All Right Mama', with 'Blue Moon of Kentucky' on the B-side, and it was tearing up the airwaves. The first time I saw Elvis, singing from a flatbed truck at a Katz drugstore opening on Lamar Avenue, two or three hundred people, mostly teenage girls, had come out to see him. With just one single to his credit, he sang those two songs over and over. That's the first time I met him... I went up to him after the show, and he invited us to his next date at the Eagle's Nest, a club promoted by Sleepy-Eyed John, the disc jockey who'd taken his name from the Merle Travis song, and was just as important as Dewey Phillips in getting Sun music out to the world."

He went on: "I remember Elvis' show at the Eagle's Nest as if were yesterday. The date was a blunder, because the place was an adult club where teenagers weren't welcome... All the same, I thought Elvis was great. He sang 'That's All Right Mama' and 'Blue Moon of Kentucky' once again (and again) plus some black blues songs and a few numbers like 'Long Tall Sally', and he didn't say much. He didn't have to, of course; his charisma alone kept everyone's attention. The thing I really noticed that night, though, was his guitar playing. Elvis was a fabulous rhythm player. He'd start into 'That's All Right Mama' with his own guitar alone, and you didn't want to hear anything else. I didn't anyway. I was disappointed when Scotty Moore and Bill Black jumped in and covered him up. Not that Scotty and Bill weren't perfect for him – the way he sounded with them that night was what I think of as seminal Presley, the sound I missed through all the years after he became so popular and made records full of orchestration and overproduction. I loved that clean, simple combination of Scotty, Bill, and Elvis with his acoustic guitar. You know, I've never heard or read anyone else praising Elvis as a rhythm guitar player, and after the Sun days

I never heard his own guitar on his records. That night at the Eagle's Nest, I remember, he was playing a Martin and he was dressed in the latest teen fashion. I think his shirt came from the National Shirt Shop, where you could get something loud and flashy or something in a good rich black for $3.98 (I did), but perhaps by then he'd started shopping at Lansky Brothers on Beale Street. If he hadn't, it wasn't long before he did. I was in there myself two or three times in '55 and '56."

Tennessee local radio latched on to the song, playing it incessantly, thanks to requests from the frankly stunned public, and then a sequence of live dates from Elvis and his band consolidated his reputation within the state. Country musician Hank Snow organised a show for Elvis at Nashville's Grand Ole Opry and his name began to be known across the USA, especially when TV appearances and widespread touring commenced in earnest. More singles, including 'Good Rockin' Tonight', built Elvis a ready fanbase, who were persuaded into purchase by the choppy, fast music and Elvis' remarkable looks and stage act (involving hip-swivelling and leg-shaking that sent girls into a frenzy and the authorities into an apoplexy).

Elvis then signed up for a year's worth of appearances on the Louisiana Hayride radio show, and met the man who was to be both his guiding light and his nemesis – Colonel Tom Parker, a manager. Parker set up a deal with RCA Victor, who took over Elvis' Sun contract for the then-vast sum of $35,000 on November 21, 1955. One of Elvis' first managers was Bob Neal, who told Rockville International in 1973: "Sam Phillips phoned me and said he had this new boy who just had a record out, and would I put him on a show. I agreed with Sam and so I got Elvis on a show on August 10th, 1954. He got a tremendous reaction, which really amazed me, because he had just started. Then a couple of months after that I was thinking one day, and asked Elvis had he got a manager. He said no and well, I said,

'I've never been a manager, but let's try it.' So I was his manager for about a year and a half."

Of the Sun studio, Neal commented: "Sam Phillips is credited with discovering a different sound, but he had been a radio engineer prior to that time and I know we had done some things on radio programs in Memphis on commercials where we used the electronic slap-back sound... Sam more or less was the first one that really capitalised on that sound on his recordings. He was also fortunate enough to see people like Elvis and Johnny Cash, Roy Orbison and Carl Perkins knocking at his door. It was like everything fitted together and clicked at the same time. Of course, a lot of people have criticised Sam about the way he drove the company business-wise. He was not quite as good a merchandiser or salesman as he could have been, because with the material he had at that time, if he had had the imagination and sales concepts that some other record people have, Sun Records might have become a big record company instead of reaching a peak and sort of staying there and dropping off."

Of the management contract being bought out by Colonel Parker, Neal said: "I had a contract with Elvis and when, through part of my efforts, Parker got interested, we had a partnership agreement. You see, I was doing quite well with my radio program in Memphis. We had a record store, a large family and I didn't really... well, I felt that Elvis was going to be very big, and I didn't want to get into the picture of being gone from town all the time. So I preferred to stay there and more or less then turned everything over to the Colonel... it was a friendly relationship all the way... I think the Colonel has done a tremendous job with Elvis. I possibly would differ a little bit with the ways he's gone down the line as far as concerts go. Elvis is always very fond of performing for a live audience and I think, possibly instead of keeping him away from an audience for so long, I might have felt that it would have been better to be back with a live audience every now and then. However, who is to argue with success, because apparently it's worked tremendously well and since he has come out to do live shows again, everything is a sell-out... so like I said, who is to argue with success?"

As for the sums involved, he recalled: "At first, when people talked to Sam it was a fairly moderate amount of money. I recall one time being on tour with Elvis out in Texas, when Mitch Miller, who was in with CBS, called, and asked about what the price was. And I told him since I had nothing to do with the record company I would simply find out and call him back. I think Sam at that time said he wanted $18,000 and I called Mitch and he laughed and laughed, because back at that time in the early 50s they were not making fantastic record deals and putting out a lot of money. Then later Colonel Parker worked on it with RCA and finally got the deal OK'd, and they paid $35,000 for the complete masters, tapes and everything, plus a $5000 bonus that went to Elvis for signing. So back at that time in late 1955, that was considered a real big deal. Sam was happy with it because he had never had a lot of money or capital, and that gave him some capital to operate with and to build and to make some investments and so on for the future."

The die was cast and Elvis' ascent to the status of music legend seemed to be assured, all in the space of 18 frantic months. Parker's first move was to get Elvis on TV, which he knew would be the best medium for true commercial success. As well as slapping his client's face and name all over a range of Presley-themed merchandise from button badges to guitars to kitchen utensils, the Colonel (an assumed rank; he had no military background) pushed Elvis onto the big TV shows of the time – CBS' Dorsey Show and the same network's Ed Sullivan Show – as well as other prime-time broadcasts. His hip-shaking act brought him notoriety and popularity in equal measure, and his records sold in vast quantities as a result. On September 9, 1956, the Sullivan show with Elvis pulled in over 80% percent of the TV audience – as many as 60 million viewers – while the Colonel pocketed a hefty sum on his behalf. Within a couple of years Parker and Elvis had signed a 50/50 contract, a ridiculously exploitative deal by today's standards.

However, some doubt was cast on this arrangement by his wife, Loanne Parker, who told Elvis Australia/EWJ (Elvis Worldwide Japan): "Colonel Parker never took 50% of Elvis' earnings, never. It's true, they did sign a contract in the 70s which was a partnership contract where they each were to receive 50%. But Colonel never collected his 50%, because it was about that time that Elvis needed extra money for his divorce settlement with Priscilla. And they were running short on funds. And Vernon said to Colonel, 'Colonel, would you just take your regular one-third for a while until we get on our feet?' Colonel took his regular third, and he never, never took 50%. Now, I'm talking about Elvis' personal appearances, I'm talking Elvis recordings and so forth – they did have an understanding that if Colonel initiated a project wherein Elvis needed to lend only his likeness or his name, that Colonel receive 50%. This would be photo albums, merchandise, things like that. Colonel conceived the ideas, Colonel followed through on the ideas. And Elvis had contributed nothing but his name and likeness, which without it, of course, would have been impossible. When those kinds of things came about, Elvis was quite willing to have Colonel take 50%."

Parker was a master at his work, which was now solely the presentation of Elvis and his products to the masses. Once Elvis' debut album, Elvis Presley, had become a huge hit in 1956 (see track-by-track analysis below), the next goal, as Parker saw it, was to establish a parallel career for his client in an entirely different arena...

This next stage in Elvis' career – as it had been for James Dean, one of Presley's idols – was to move into films, with a multi-picture studio deal that earned him millions with a percentage of the box-office take. The first, Love Me Tender (1956), and others such as Jailhouse Rock (1957) and King Creole (1958) are regarded today as the best of a bad bunch: the Presley movie canon was viewed as doubly guilty for being cheap rubbish in their own right (in the end the studio had perfected the art of shooting and editing a film in just 17 days!) and also for degrading Elvis' massive talents from the status of hotshot rock'n'roll provocateur to family-friendly bubblegum puppet.

However, Elvis' movie career could have been so different: he was offered the chance to audition in The Godfather, Cat on a Hot Tin Roof, The Defiant Ones, Midnight Cowboy, A Star Is Born with Barbra Streisand and West Side Story – but Colonel Parker advised against them. (As it turned out, all these films provided Academy Awards for the actors that starred in them.)

As Red West said of the Presley films: "I enjoyed the first ones. Blue Hawaii, GI Blues, Flaming Star especially. I could count on one hand the ones that were good, and the rest of them were things that were thrown at him with no thought of anything other than making a buck. Forget the songs were bad, the scripts were bad, but for those of you who saw Wild in the Country and those movies I just mentioned, he had the ability if he'd had some training, and also he could have done better in the others. He just kinda breezed through the others to get them out of the way, because there was nothing to them as far as he was concerned. I mean, Wild in the Country was some of the best acting without a doubt he ever did, and the one in New Orleans – King Creole – those were two."

Colonel Tom Parker is in many ways the keystone of the Elvis story, just as Sam Phillips and Gladys Presley were when it came to determining the way their prodigy would progress through life. Born in 1909, and thus a full generation older than Elvis, Parker was actually a Dutch-born immigrant to the States named Andreas Cornelius van Kuijk, although he maintained a lie about a West Virginia upbringing until relatives in Holland recognised him in a photo with Elvis. He had worked as a dog catcher and pet cemetery manager in the 1940s before moving into the dark waters of artist management.

As his wife Loanne later told Elvis Australia/EWJ, Parker was devoted to furthering Elvis' career at all costs: "Colonel was business from morning til night, 24 hours a day. He thought about Elvis and his business. He just didn't turn it off. It kept going. He expected everyone to be as dedicated as he was. And that made it a little tough on some of his people, because they needed some private life. And it was tough for them to get it... Colonel never stopped thinking about Elvis. Never stopped thinking about what he could do. He was a perfectionist. If the billboards looked good this engagement, how could he make them look better the next engagement. He never stopped. We would be driving around, and he would say, 'Now that board, that's a good location. But I don't think we'll use it the next time. We're going for a better location.' His focus was, what can I do to better present Elvis? What can I do to better protect Elvis when it comes to contracts and business affairs? What can I do to let the people know in a better way that Elvis is going to be there? He never stopped thinking about it, ever. Never. He had a very unusual mind. Most people have one voice of inner dialogue. It's our inner thought. We think all the time, words are formulated in our minds. That's our thinking process. Colonel had multi levels of inner dialogue. And I'm saying that these occurred simultaneously. It's something that I realised finally, after being around him 24 hours a day, year in, year out. I've met a few people since that time that are similar, but I've never known anyone who had more than one inner dialogue at a time in their mind. So, where I might think about one subject, and I might think about different subjects, skipping back and forth, Colonel could think about a dozen things simultaneously. And he did that all the time…"

Getting back to the films, at a rare press conference in Canada in 1957, Elvis talked in his usual reserved style about the acting process, saying: "Well, there's nobody who helps you out. They have a director and a producer. As far as the acting and as far as the singing and all, you're on your own. I mean, nobody tells you how to do that, you have to learn it yourself…that's something you learn through experience. I think that maybe I might accomplish something at it through the years… In some scenes, I was pretty natural. And in others I was trying to act. And when you start trying to act, you're dead."

And on the music front, Elvis' rise to the top wasn't unhindered: the USA's political-religious axis was a powerful enemy, and in no time the establishment lined up, eager to take Elvis down. His show at the Mississippi-Alabama Fair in 1956 was attended by no fewer than 100 National Guardsmen (America's domestic military force) in order to prevent a horde of hysterical teenagers from destroying the event.

But the music just kept coming. A milestone event occurred on 4 December 1956 when a jam session occurred with the so-called Million Dollar Quartet – Elvis, Carl Perkins, Jerry Lee Lewis and Johnny Cash. All four men jammed on as many as 40 country and R&B standards. Of this remarkable event, Cash wrote: "There's certainly a sense that Carl Perkins stands in the shadow of Elvis, Jerry Lee, and me. You can see when people talk or write about the so-called Million Dollar Quartet session, the only time to my knowledge that all four of us sang together. Somehow Carl's name always seems to come last in the list of participants, but in fact it was his session that day. Nobody else was booked into the studio. I was there – I was the first to arrive and the last to leave, contrary to what has been written. I was just there to watch Carl record, which he did until mid-afternoon, when Elvis came in with his girlfriend. At that point the session stopped and we all started laughing and cutting up together.

Then Elvis sat down at the piano, and we started singing gospel songs we all knew, then some Bill Monroe songs."

He went on: "Elvis wanted to hear songs Bill had written besides 'Blue Moon of Kentucky', and I knew the whole repertoire. So, again contrary to what some people have written, my voice is on the tape. It's not obvious, because I was farthest away from the mike and I was singing a lot higher than I usually did in order to stay in key with Elvis, but I guarantee you, I'm there. I forget exactly when Jerry Lee came in, but I remember clearly when Elvis invited him to take over at the piano and he launched into 'Vacation in Heaven'. That was the first time I ever heard Jerry Lee, and I was bowled over. He was so great that the next thing I remember, Elvis and his girlfriend were gone. The thing I remember after that, apart from going next door for coffee and cheeseburgers, is seeing the now famous Million Dollar Quartet photo in the Memphis Commercial Appeal and wondering what happened to Elvis' girlfriend. She'd been sitting on the piano when the photo was taken."

He concluded: "If you're wondering why Elvis left right after Jerry Lee got started, the answer is simple: nobody, not even Elvis, ever wanted to follow Jerry Lee. And no, I don't remember Jerry Lee ever saying anything disparaging about Elvis. He didn't have an attitude about Elvis especially; he just had an attitude."

The same year, promoters and preachers joined forces across the States to try and prevent Elvis from playing, or at least to get him to tone down his act. At one show in Jacksonville, Florida, a local juvenile court judge labelled him a "savage" and promised to arrest him if he did his on-stage act: in response, Presley stood still during the performance – while waggling a finger to and fro. The singer Hank Ballard once commented, "In white society, the movement of the butt, the shaking of the leg, all that was considered obscene. Now here's this white boy grinding and rolling his belly and shaking that notorious leg. I hadn't even seen the black dudes doing that."

But by 1957 the puritanical censorship had gone away, because the commercial power of the Presley name crushed all attempts to gag him. If a promoter refused to let him play, his fans drove 12 hours to see him play in another venue. If mainstream radio turned up its nose at his records, kids just tuned into the new breed of rock'n'roll stations on their new transistor radios (sales of which jumped by 5000% from 1955 to '58). Then major TV and radio sponsors ploughed huge amounts of money into advertising on rock'n'roll shows, lending serious commercial weight to the scene.

Country star Waylon Jennings remembered meeting the King at this stage: "I got to meet Elvis in Lubbock. Even then, he was about the hottest thing to hit West Texas. They invited me backstage, gave me free tickets, and the whole show was there. He and Scotty Moore were standing over by the stage, and Elvis was just jumping around everywhere, bouncing and bubbling over with enthusiasm, full of more energy than anybody I ever saw. He was talking to me like he'd known me a thousand years. 'I'll sing you my next thing I'm going to record', he said. It was 'Tweedle Dee', the LaVern Baker song. 'My next single', though I don't think he ever recorded it. He did it on the show that night... I was crazy about Elvis. I loved that churning rhythm on the bottom. He didn't even have drums yet, but the rock'n'roll part was unmistakable. You'd think it was overnight, but he'd been plugging away a long time. He had a hard way to go, because they were fighting him from every corner in the South, calling him names – white trash bebop nigger stuff; though he could pretty well handle himself. We had met formally only a couple of times, mostly in Las Vegas at the tail end of the 60s. RCA invited me to see his show, and he asked me back to visit him. He knew who I was; he called me hillbilly."

And so Elvis' career progressed. Helped along by a cynical industry keen to find a broader market for its underground sound, Presley took a handful of black music, cleaned it up for public consumption and repackaged it as the negro R&B it was safe for white people to like. To this day there are many critics who view him a puppet of his paymasters, exploited so that a new kind of music would make them megabucks. Elvis was a musician and performer of great power and skill – but there's no doubting that he played black music developed by a class of artists ignored and suppressed by the mainstream for their skin colour.

As he explained at the Canada press conference in 1957, the success of the formula meant that he no longer had much privacy: "Well, let's face the facts. Anybody that's in the public eye, their life is never private. I mean, anything you do, the public knows about it. And that's the way it's always been, that's the way it'll always be… I've been scratched and bitten [by fans]… I just accept it with a broad mind because actually they don't intend to hurt you. I mean, it's not that. They want pieces of you for souvenirs, is all. A crowd of people can hurt you and not even realise they're doing it… When I'm travelling around, I don't go anywhere. I just eat in the room… Naturally, you can't go places like other people. You can't go to ball games. You can't go to the local theatre and things like that. Like, back at home, whenever I want to see a movie, well I have the theatre manager show it to me after the theatre closes up at night. We have a fairgrounds there, and I rent the fairgrounds after it closes up sometimes."

Once, the adulation of the fans got so violent that Colonel Parker physically removed him from the scene, despite a painful back that had plagued him since his youth. As Loanne remembered the incident: "When the Colonel was a young man… in Holland, one of his jobs was carrying big rounds of cheese from the factory onto the barges that would carry this cheese on to its destination. And he said they were extremely heavy, like 150 pounds or something. And he felt that during his formative years, he was maybe 13, 14 years old, that he hurt his back during that time. That was the start. Because he had back problems all of his life. But when they were filming That's the Way It Is at the International Hotel, I was sitting in Colonel's booth with Colonel, and they had a runway, it was going out into the audience. And at one point Elvis was singing and going on the runway out into the audience, and Colonel looked around. He always sat right on the outside of the booth so he could slip out at any minute. He looked around and he said, 'He's gonna get in trouble'. The fans from the back had started to move forward and he was about to be mobbed. And Colonel jumped up, ran up, picked up Elvis and put him on the other side of the barrier. And I sat there. I just, I absolutely could not believe it. He came back, sat down like nothing had happened, and I said, 'Colonel, your back. Are you all right?' And he said, 'I had to help him'. It was that simple. He didn't think. He just did it… At personal appearances, Colonel would sit in front of the stage. And he always was watching the audience to see what was happening with the audience. He knew Elvis was taking care of his show on stage. That wasn't his business. His business was to protect Elvis, to make sure that things didn't get out of hand."

As Red West told Todd Slaughter: "Even in Las Vegas… people like Frank Sinatra, many of the stars, Sammy Davis – they could go out and pretty well mingle. They could go down if they wanted to gamble or whatever. People didn't bother them too much. But Elvis tried it – once – and the whole casino... everybody stopped playing and came around just to watch and see what he was doing, and he could not get out and do what most people do, and everything had to be at night. And still, I mean, back in Memphis he would rent movie theaters at night because he couldn't go to a regular movie, but still the gate in front of the house was always crowded with fans and they would follow and they would be at the movie when it was over, and it was constant. We were always trying to find different ways to go places, but he didn't want to hurt anybody's feelings. He did wish he had a little more privacy... When he started making the movies it became even more evident, became more of a visual thing that people would come around to see him, and that's when it really started that he couldn't even go out the gate and we'd go the back way out, jump over the fence, whatever. But when the movies started, after Love Me Tender, it became pretty hard to go out in public."

Interestingly for such a young man – he was only 22 at this stage – Elvis had a mature view on the insane events around him, picking out the high and low points: "Well, I'm happier now in a lot of ways. And in some ways, I mean, I was having a lot of fun then, you know... It has its advantages, and disadvantages... I like movies better than I do TV work. If you goof in movies, you can just go back and take it over. In TV, you just goof. There's no going back and taking it over."

As for Vernon and Gladys, Presley added: "They're just like they've always been, I mean as far as being themselves. But it is kind of a strain on them, because, you know, people never leave them alone, to be truthful about it." This had spilled over into violence when it came to his own situation, Elvis admitted, saying that he had been involved in fights. "Somebody hitting me or trying to hit me... I mean, I can take all the, you know, I can take ridicule and slander, and I've been called names you know right to my face and everything – that I can take. But I've had a few guys who try to take a swing at me and naturally you can't just stand there, you've got to do something."

Women began to pay more attention to Elvis, of course. Joe Esposito recalled Anita Wood, Elvis' first girlfriend, to the writer Lea Fryman with the words: "They dated for a while after Elvis got back to the States, but when Priscilla came to Graceland they stopped seeing each other. Today she lives in Texas and refuses to give interviews. I don't blame her. Recently a collector paid $8000 for a love letter Elvis wrote to Anita. She doesn't know how the letter got to Christie's, because she burnt all Elvis' letters before she got married in 1964."

When Anita Wood was still giving interviews, she recalled their first date, saying: "Lamar [Fike, Elvis' associate] called and said, 'Elvis would like to meet you tonight'. Well, I had a date, and so I wouldn't break it. And Lamar went ballistic. I will never forget that… 'You won't go with Elvis Presley? Break your date'. But I couldn't do that. So I didn't go. And I didn't think I would ever hear from him again, but I did…. We were a Southern family, you know, so he came to the door to pick me up. We went out in the limousine. And Elvis was driving. And we drove around Memphis a lot, we stopped by a hamburger place, and he sent Lamar in for I don't know how many dozens of hamburgers, lots of them, and he and Lamar ate every one of them. And then we went to Graceland. He had just bought Graceland, and he wanted to show me Graceland, and we went out there."

As to whether the King attempted to woo his new girlfriend physically, she added: "He tried. He wanted me to go upstairs and see his bedroom and his big magnificent bed, which I did. And we walked in the bedroom. And it was a huge bed, I mean, the biggest bed I've ever seen, bar none, even now. A huge bed. And then he tried to make a little move on me. And I said, no, really, I have to go home now. So he took me home. And that was the first date we had. He was a gentleman about it. He took me home… He was my first love. I met him when I was 19 years old, and I came from a very conservative family and I'd never gone steady or anything. So of course when I met Elvis, I did fall in love with him, and he did with me. We had a wonderful time, great fun together. I loved the guy. And it was just great, like a family."

However, Elvis' later spell in the army put paid to the relationship, as she explained: "He went to Germany, and while he was there, of course he met Priscilla, who was… a pretty young girl at 14. But when he came back, we still continued to

date. And of course, you know, Elvis could make you believe anything in the world, so he had me believing that she was just a friend and her daddy was in the Army with him, and there was nothing to it whatsoever."

Of Elvis' many other female companions, Esposito recalled: "So many of his female fans were so eager just to meet him... I suppose in a way, I made many girls' dreams come true. And because Elvis was so famous, he couldn't just go out on a normal

date. Everything was arranged to the finest detail. I don't feel bad, because it was not bad. Most of the time, Elvis would just sit around with three or four girls and read to them in his hotel suite. I think he just needed to be reminded that his fans still loved him. And still do..."

It's a measure of the success of the white-boy-plays-black-songs approach of Elvis and his successors (Bill Haley, Jerry Lee Lewis, Buddy Holly, Gene Vincent in the US and Cliff Richard, Tommy Steele, Billy Fury and the Beatles in the UK) that rock'n'roll and rockabilly were global phenomena by the early 1960s. Meanwhile, the early black artists who had provided the inspiration for it all – Fats Domino, Wynonie Harris, Big Joe Turner, Etta James, Big Mama Thornton (who first recorded Elvis' hit 'Hound Dog') and others – were reduced to B-league status or forgotten entirely. In the hall of fame of rock'n'roll, the only black artists to make it to the status of real legends were Chuck Berry and Little Richard – the former because he used a heavier, guitar-based approach (which inspired later musicians such as Jimi Hendrix) and the latter because he controversially sang about "tutti-frutti", a slang expression for a gay man, in a searing, shrieked vocal style. No wonder Little Richard's fans referred to him as 'The Real King of Rock'n'Roll'.

All this tied in with the rise of the teenager, a demographic that had been hardly acknowledged before the war. Now that the kids had money – a result of increased affluence as America's economy got back on track – they had buying power and thus commercial importance. Suddenly there was a large divide between what the teenagers wanted and what their parents wanted them to have, a generation gap which is the norm today – but which scared the hell out of society's moral guardians back then.

As Elvis told the press conference in Las Vegas in 1969, "In 1956 I met Colonel Sanders", and laughed before adding,

"Parker, I mean Parker. He arranged to have me go on television… So they put me on television. And the whole thing broke loose. It was wild. I tell you for sure. I did the Ed Sullivan show four times. I did the Steve Allen show. I did the Jackie Gleason show. They had me singing to a dog and filmed me from [the waist] up… All the time, they were telling me, 'Hey! You! Stand still! Stand still!' And they kept asking me, where are you from, white boy? I told them, Memphis. They thought, he's a dummy, we'll just put him in back… The first time I auditioned for the Arthur Godfrey talent show they turned me down! They said, 'Man, get him outta here! Get him out!' They took that jerk-off, instead… Pat Boone, yeah, it was Pat. That was OK by me, 'cause he had a pretty good voice... Anyway, later on they sent me to Hollywood. To make movies. It was all new to me. I was only 21 years old... When they yelled 'action', I didn't know what to do… I made four movies, and in 1958, I got drafted... I went into the army and stayed a couple of years. That was loads-a-fun... They made a big deal outta cuttin' all my hair off and all that jazz."

At the peak of his career – and the rock'n'roll boom – Elvis received his draft letter for a two-year service with the United States Army. Although fans had requested that he be exempt from national service or be treated differently from the other soldiers, he was regarded as a common trooper – although the cutting of his hair and sideburns was a media event rather unlike that of the average grunt. Charlie Hodge, Elvis' harmony singer and friend, told Lea Fryman of Elvis Presley News: "I remember one time when we were all out sleeping, eating and living in three feet of snow, some colonel came up to Elvis and said, we're going to fly you out to Miami to a large convention, then you'll be taken to Paris to meet the Pope. Elvis looked at the colonel and said, 'Sir, there's 15,000 men out there who, like me, are sleeping out in the snow – and for me to leave them and get this special treatment, then having to come back and look these guys in the face... sir, I just couldn't do that."

Elvis then spent two years in Germany, where he rose to the rank of sergeant and met his future wife, the then 14-year-old Priscilla Beaulieu. He returned to the United States on March 2, 1960, and was honourably discharged. In 2003 Priscilla Presley appeared on CNN's Larry King Show, recalling the early days of her relationship with Elvis: "You have to remember that when I met Elvis, you know, it wasn't the fanfare that it is today or even when he was here in the states and I was in Germany growing up. So I saw him at a very vulnerable time. He had just lost his mother and he was grieving. And I came into his life and he somehow, you know, felt like confiding in me and talking to me and I was like a sounding board for him as a 14-year-old kid... I didn't realise at that time how serious it was. You know, I had my mother and my father convincing me that he would be going back to Hollywood and he'd be back with the actresses and dating them and that he wasn't serious about me at all. So I had him saying one thing to me and my parents telling me something else... Well, they didn't know how serious it was between us. They, you know, they were very fond of him. They were very fond of his father... I was 16, 17 at the time. At that time, girls got married. They weren't thinking of a career. So, Elvis was very convincing to my parents and saying, I'll take good care of her. Please let her come... So my parents let me come. They let me go to school." Lisa-Marie Presley was born in 1968, nine months to the day after Priscilla and Elvis' wedding.

By the early years of the 60s, Elvis was evolving a world of his own, ensconced away from public view in the huge Memphis mansion he called Graceland and surrounding himself with a bunch of yes-men referred to as the Memphis Mafia. Their logo, TCB, referred to 'Taking care of business' and aptly reflected the

Presley phenomenon's ability to pull in and consume enormous amounts of money, with little attention paid to taste or style. Where was the rebellion now?

One member of the Memphis Mafia, Marty Lacker, told Larry King: "Elvis dressed in very flashy clothes, which was different than the kids back then. Most of the guys back then wore crew cuts and Levis and T-shirts. And Elvis wore flashy clothes, wore his collar up, his hair was a lot longer than the rest of the people. And basically, I dressed the same way, coming from New York. And the kids used to kid us about who was going to outdress who the next day. He sang in a couple of talent shows in Memphis… at the school. But it really wasn't known back then except for people who were close to him."

Of the accusation that the Memphis Mafia were merely a bunch of yes-men and hangers-on, Lacker once said: "We've been called every name in the book, but we've been called those names by people who have no understanding what that relationship was about… It was a close brotherhood. Elvis didn't have one best friend, he had about nine of them. And those were basically the guys from the early years. And we grew up together. We were like brothers. The people who make statements like that, I mean, we just smile and laugh, because they have no idea what it was all about."

Lamar Fike told Larry King about the trials of working with the King: "We were there mainly to kind of keep everything together. At times we didn't, but it was still fun trying… At times, [he was] very difficult, but most of the time, he was a lot of fun. You know, you're around somebody like him 24 hours a day, and you have to watch what you're doing because you become a little too familiar and you say things you shouldn't and sometimes you get in arguments. And it was a constant amount of pressure. It never really stopped. It kept you on your toes… When he got hard nosed, you knew he was there. He

could make it hard on you. It's just like I said, it's hard to really separate the lines. You're friends and you're an employee and you're all the above. My thing was we just fought all the time. And I always lost. I got fired about 500 times. But it's all part of it."

Another associate, Jerry Schilling, told Larry King of the formation of the Memphis Mafia: "We used to go to Vegas and wear mohair suits and carry guns. And the press kind of affectionately started saying, the Memphis Mafia is back in town. And we kind of liked it. We were young guys… Probably over the years, there's been about 12, 13 guys… he didn't go out and hire people because they were an accountant or a tour manager, he hired people that he trusted and then you worked into the position."

Patty Perry, a junior associate of the Memphis Mafia, said: "We were a family. Elvis was a prisoner of his own fame. We were the ones that always hung out with him. I mean, he couldn't go anywhere, there were like 20 girls outside the gate, 24/7. But we were his family. And we had so much fun together. And these guys were his best friends… I loved him. He was an incredible man. You know he had guys that worked with him who were Italian, he had Jewish guys, he had Christian guys. And he always wore a Jewish star and a cross, because he didn't want to get shot out of heaven on a technicality. I mean, he was a funny man. We were his friends. You know, we were it. And all he asked back was our friendship and loyalty."

She added: "Elvis didn't celebrate just regular holidays. Elvis would give you gifts off the cuff. You know, if he went to the jewellery store, everybody got something. If he got a car, everybody got one. If he got motorcycles, everybody got one. What made him happy was to see the look on your face when he gave you that gift. It wasn't the gift itself."

Jerry Schilling recalled Elvis' generosity with the words: "He didn't talk about it. But I think he knew that I lost my mother when I was a year old. We grew up in the same neighbourhood, [a] poor part of Memphis. And in 1974, he said, 'You know, you never had a home. I want to be the one to give it to you.' And nobody knew about it. The guys knew about it, but you know, it wasn't for publicity. And I still live there and I'll always live there."

But the generosity was, as any psychologist would suggest, perhaps a way of covering up another emotion – such as regret or embarrassment – as Marty Lacker implied: "Elvis was a complex and contradictory type of person. I mean, he had many sides to him. Elvis could not really bring himself to say 'I'm sorry' to anybody. If he got mad at them or did something that he knew he shouldn't have done, he'd get over it in 30 minutes. But... instead of saying I'm sorry, instead of saying I'm sorry, he'd buy you something... the only time I ever heard him say I'm sorry, he said it to me because of an argument, the one and only argument we ever had. And it shocked me when he did it, because he just didn't do that. He'd go buy you something."

Elvis was known for being polite to a fault. At the Canada press conference in 1957, he couldn't be quick enough to pay homage to a host of shark-like industry figures when discussing the reasons for his success: "I mean, well, if disc jockeys didn't play it, the people couldn't hear it, so they couldn't know what was happening, you know. I contribute it to a little bit of everything. I contribute it largely to the people that have accepted me, and then the disc jockeys, and the good handling that I've had, the management and everything." This naïve trait led to some strange habits, including the purchase of dozens of unnecessary cars ("I'm just now realizing how extravagant it was. Because I have too many. I mean, nobody drives them. They sit up and they get stale. The tyres go down on 'em. Actually, I have no need for them... I just went crazy...") and clothes: "I'll tell you what I did the other day. I have, I had, a German-made Messerschmitt, a little car. And there's a guy there in town who has been wanting that Messerschmitt for the last year. And so, he owns a clothing store, one of the top clothing stores in Memphis. So I went up there the other day, and I told him, I said, 'You've been wanting the car so bad', I said, 'I'll make a deal with you'. He said okay, and I said, 'You let me pick out all the clothes in here that I want and you can have the car.' So I was up there for about two hours and a half, and the store was a wreck when I left."

The films he continued to make were responsible for much of Presley's decline in the early 1960s, as well as the rise of newer, hipper groups such as the Beatles, Stones, Kinks and the other members of the British Invasion. According to Priscilla's later autobiography, Elvis "blamed his fading popularity on his humdrum movies. He loathed their stock plots and short shooting schedules. He could have demanded better, more substantial scripts, but he didn't. [He] continued to make the movies and record the dismal soundtracks, putting forth less effort with each new release. Artistically speaking, no one blamed him. The scripts were all the same, the songs progressively worse."

However, on December 3, 1968, Elvis starred in an NBC-broadcast concert later labelled The '68 Comeback Special, so named because it marked a turning-point in his fortunes. In recent years he had begun to suffer from weight gain, marring his lithe figure and leading many to mock him. However, for this show he had shed the excess pounds and was encased in a leather suit for one of his finest performances ever. The following year he began the first of over 1000 shows in Las Vegas, where he performed for many years. After seven years in the commercial doldrums, the single 'Suspicious Minds' topped the Billboard charts on November 1, 1969.

Of the song, Waylon Jennings said: "Felton Jarvis at RCA

really cared about Elvis. He produced 'Suspicious Minds', which may be the best record Elvis ever cut, and one time he called me up to see if I could help. 'He likes you', Felton said to me. 'Do you think you could get him interested in music again?' I told him I didn't know, and that the only way you could find out was by getting all those yes people away from him and letting him go somewhere and hang out and play music. He might get interested, because I truly believed Elvis liked to sing… Elvis had changed the world and now he was gone. Maybe he didn't have as much impact on me as Hank Williams or George Jones or Buddy, but most of us marked time as Before Elvis and After Elvis."

Session horns player Wayne Jackson told Elvis Worldwide Australia/Elvis Worldwide Japan about the 'Suspicious Minds' sessions and the run-up to those legendary recordings: "Elvis liked our band, the Mar-Keys, because we had horns. We were an all white band singing rhythm and blues. He was at that time singing 'Teddy Bear', I guess, right at about '60, '61, '62. But he would come out to where we were playing and sit in his car, right behind the bandstand, and listen to the band. We'd go out and talk to him during the breaks. Sometimes we'd go to his house or go somewhere late at night after our gig. So I had a friendship with him as far back as 1960. That was my first experience with him. We were teenagers and we were big little stars. Our first record, 'Last Night', was a No. 1 record. That was where it started, and then over the years there were brief contacts with Elvis through hanging around Memphis and being with other people in Memphis like T.G. Shepherd or Ronnie Angel. Occasionally, there would be a foray out to his house or something. So there was a contact through the 60s up until Andrew and I recorded with him at American [studios]."

He went on: "Andrew Love and I were just there making records when Elvis came through. We were doing all the records at American studios with Chips Moman, the producer. Andrew and I did all the horn work. We did Neil Diamond, Wilson Pickett, Dionne Warwick. We did everybody over there. At that time, Neil Diamond was more important than Elvis because Neil had a lot of current hit records and he was the big star of the time. Elvis had been doing movies. Let's face it, at that time, to a certain crowd, he wasn't really a musical giant, he was more of a matinee movie star idol. When he came into American, though, we made records. During those sessions, Elvis was welded to a great group of musicians, writers and producers who were all in one spot. There he was face up to it and he was wonderful. He just sang great. I think these sessions took him over into the real genuine big-time musical giant that he really was. It was really fun and exciting to have him there."

Jackson thought that Elvis was in good spirits at this point in his career, saying: "I think that was a period in Elvis' life when he was having a pretty good time. He realised that the songs were better than the songs he had had handed to him. The songs were serious. The first time I heard him sing 'In The Ghetto' I was sitting with my horn looking at the music. I hadn't heard any of it yet. We were playing around with it, seeing what was what. When I heard the tune I just thought, 'Oh, my God, this is wonderful. This is it. Elvis is capable of this.' I knew that was going to be a landmark record for him because it was about a very current topic. It was serious, a heavy deal. How serious is 'Teddy Bear' or 'Jailhouse Rock'? You know what I mean? This was serious stuff, and I knew that it was pivotal music for him. He did too. 'Suspicious Minds' was a topical subject for him at that time I believe lyrically, and 'In The Ghetto' was a topical subject. We were in the ghetto literally. American Studios was in the worst part of town. Stax, American, and Hi, all three were in the worst part of town. So we were in the ghetto and he had that piece of material, and I think he really felt that. It was a

thrill to be involved in those songs knowing in my mind that they were as important to his career as they were. His attitude was great, by the way. We were playing poker upstairs and they were cutting tracks downstairs. We would come down, and he'd be singing. We'd put the horns in with the track. He liked that. He liked to sing with the horns and hear all that. Sometimes the background vocals would be in the room too."

Things were looking up. Of his career, Elvis told the press conference in Las Vegas in 1969: "The next thing I knew, I was out of the service and making movies, again… I did some good pictures that did very well for me, like Blue Hawaii... and some pretty forgettable ones too! I sure lost my musical direction in Hollywood. My songs were the same conveyor-belt mass production, just like most of my movies were... Now I'm back and on the right road. Those movies sure got me into a rut. I want to make amends. I really missed working live, in front of an audience, that's why I'm here..."

In 1965 Elvis met The Beatles, a band who were coming close to making him look obsolete. His close associate Joe Esposito recalled the historic meeting in GQ magazine in 2000 with the words: "There's a lot of different versions of this story… When the Beatles first came to the United States, I think it was 1964. They wanted to meet Elvis and it never worked out. So in 1965 when they came back again, Brian Epstein and Colonel Parker got together and talked about seeing if they could arrange a meeting. Basically what it was, they said fine. Elvis was making a movie at the time. I forgot which one it was. And we were at MGM studios and their road manager, Mal Evans, nice man, he was the biggest Elvis fan in the world. I mean he was amazing, a bigger fan even than the Beatles were. So Malcolm came over to the studio to meet the Colonel and he was all dressed up nice in his suit and tie, and everything like that. So Colonel Parker called me on the set, and he said, 'Joe, I need to talk to you'. So I went over to the Colonel's office. He introduces Malcolm. And he said, 'Take Malcolm over to the set to meet Elvis and talk about what night we're going to get together'. And I said, 'Great'. So I took Malcolm over there. He was a nervous wreck, the poor guy. I mean, he was just shaking in his boots, I mean. You know, when somebody meets somebody they idolize, they don't know what to say, they can't talk. And I introduced Malcolm to Elvis and he was so nervous he shook his hand and that was it. There was nothing to say. You know, say something Malcolm, you know. But he just said how much he admired Elvis, and the Beatles are really anxious to meet him and all of that."

He went on: "What happened is that Colonel Parker and myself had two limousines pick us up at Elvis' house. At the house was Elvis and Priscilla, and my wife Joan and a bunch of the guys' girlfriends and wives and stuff... the boys had a house rented up on Coldwater Canyon. We went up there – two limousines – we went inside, met the guys and a couple of their friends with them. Got in the limousines. Colonel was with John and Paul in one limousine. I was with Ringo and George Harrison in the other car and a couple of other guys, Malcolm the road manager. And we all go back to the house. The Colonel, you know, being the promoter that he is, he leaked it out that the Beatles are meeting Elvis tonight. So we get out there and there's thousands of kids hanging all over the walls, climbing the trees, and reporters. And we pull in, go into the driveway and all the boys get out and we went to the door and Elvis was there to greet them... they were introduced and Brian Epstein and people like that all walked in to the living room – the family room. And the TV was on – Elvis always had a television on – all the time. I don't care what it was, it was always on. It was like his company, I guess. So we sat down and they talked for a little while. It was really quiet. They all just sat there and looked at Elvis. They didn't know what to say. The same thing I told you about before. I've met big stars too, and I didn't know what to say either. So they're the same way. And like John Lennon said, 'If it wasn't for Elvis Presley, there would be no Beatles'. So they idolised this guy. And that's where Elvis got up off the couch and he said, 'Well, if these guys are all going to sit around and look at me, I'm going to sleep'. And they said, 'No Elvis, we're sorry! We didn't know what to say. Let's sit down and talk and relax'. Then they went and got a couple of acoustic guitars and sat around and started playing some old songs. You know oldies-but-goodies songs – Chuck Berry tunes and just some instrumentals... everything was a real quiet evening. Very nice. It was polite. It lasted for about two or three hours and there were no cameras, – no pictures taken whatsoever. People say there's pictures. No recordings, nothing like that. The only pictures of that meeting were outside taken by fans and photographers. Nothing on the inside. No pictures taken of them together. And it was great. It was real enjoyable. They were real nice guys."

As John Lennon later put it: "It was nice meeting Elvis. He was just Elvis, you know? He seemed normal to us, and we were asking about his making movies and not doing any personal appearances or TV. I asked him if he was preparing new ideas for his next film and he drawled, 'Ah sure am. Ah play a country boy with a guitar who meets a few gals along the way, and ah sing a few songs'. We all looked at one another. Finally Presley and Colonel Parker laughed and explained that the only time they departed from that formula – for Wild in the Country – they lost money... In front of the TV, he had a massive amplifier with a bass plugged into it, and he was up playing bass all the time with the picture up on the TV. So we just got in there and played with him. We all plugged in whatever was around, and we played and sang. He had a jukebox, like I do, but I think he had all his hits on it. But if I'd made as many as him, maybe I'd have all mine on."

Paul McCartney recalled of the meeting: "He was our greatest idol, but the styles were changing in favour of us. He was a pretty powerful image to British people… the great thing for me [was] that he was into the bass, so there I was, 'Well, let me show you a thing or two, El…' Suddenly he was a mate. It was a great conversation piece for me. I could actually talk about the bass, and we sat around and just enjoyed ourselves. He was great – talkative and friendly and a little bit shy. But that was his image. We expected that, we hoped for that. It was one of the great meetings of my life. I think he liked us. I think at that time, he may have felt a little bit threatened, but he didn't say anything. We certainly didn't feel any antagonism. These were great times, so even if you didn't enjoy all of the events that much, you could still go home to Liverpool and say, 'Well, you know who I met?'"

David Stanley was Elvis' very young stepbrother after Vernon married Dee, and recalled on the Larry King show: "I moved into the Graceland Mansion in 1960 after my mother, who was divorced, married Elvis' widowed father. So, when I met Elvis Presley, I didn't know what a hound dog was, I didn't know what 'the King' meant. And it was funny, when I met Elvis, I met most of these guys. I mean, Marty Lacker and Lamar Fike, I mean, you know, this is like a little hoe-down down South with the family. And, you know, I walked in, and I was the little four-year-old snotty kid who just couldn't comprehend what was going on. But I did understand one thing – I came from a boarding-house home and moved into Graceland. And I thought, this is going to be a great ride. And it really was. It was a great ride. It was a lot of good friends and a bonding. We stood up for each other, we took up for each other. And it's so cool to see my buddies and all of us get together and talk about Elvis and

celebrate Elvis' birthday... I got a lot of attention being driven to school in a pink Cadillac every day, I mean, when Elvis is your big brother. He was more like a father figure. He was 20 years older than I was. He taught me everything. He taught me music. He taught me how to be [cool]. If there's any cool there, it came from Elvis. He taught me about girls. He taught me about spiritual matters. And all the other individuals involved. It wasn't just Elvis. You know, we're like those veterans, like World War II or Korean veterans or Vietnam veterans, we all experienced this unique thing."

He went on: "He was very generous to me... you know, my father was swept out of my life when I was a kid. My mother and father divorced in '59. When I moved into Graceland with my two older brothers, I came in with Elvis's new stepmother, Dee, who was my mother, and Elvis was a little reluctant towards my mother, because he had just lost his own mother. But he looked over at me and he picked me up and he gave me a hug and he welcomed me into his family. And he took me in and he shared his life with me. He knew that my dad had been swept out of my life, and he did that replacement thing... He was so silent about that. He went the extra mile to make you feel special. You know, there are a few people in the world that can pat you on the back and you're good for another 10,000 miles."

While in Vegas Elvis struck up a lifelong friendship with Tom Jones, who had been inspired to launch his own career by Elvis' early rhythm and blues records. As Jones told the BBC, "The first time I met Elvis was in Los Angeles in 1965. My first successful year. I'd met all the British groups first, because I did British television before I went to America, so meeting The Beatles and The Rolling Stones and all these famous bands at the time was great in itself. Then I go to America and I meet Elvis Presley. And the first meeting was, I went to Paramount studios in Hollywood to talk about a song for a movie, and they said 'Elvis is here today filming and he would like to meet you'. So I thought, my God, I didn't know that he knew that I existed, because I had three singles out and one album at the time. And that was 'It's Not Unusual', 'What's New Pussycat' and a ballad called 'With These Hands'."

He went on: "When I go on the set where Elvis was filming, he got out of his helicopter. It was like a mock helicopter for the film, and he walks towards me and he's singing 'With These Hands', which was my record. I couldn't believe it. It was like a dream, that Elvis Presley was singing my song, you know, to me! We had a picture taken, and he said to me, 'How the hell do you sing like that?' And I said, 'Well, you are partly to blame, you know, listening to your records in the 50s'. He said, 'What's it like in Wales then? You come from Wales?' I said 'Yeah'. And he said, 'Do all people sing like that in Wales?' I said, 'Well, not exactly', but I said, 'Welsh people have strong voices, that is where I get my strength from. My volume is where I come from, but I was influenced more by American music than I was Welsh traditional music. It's a combination. I have a Welsh voice, but because of American music influencing me so much, I am sounding like I do'. Because they thought I was black, you know. When they first started playing my records in America, they thought I was black. And so did Elvis Presley. He said, 'When I heard 'What's New Pussycat', I thought it was a black fella singing it'. Which was strange for him to say because they thought he was black when he started. We became friends from that day on, and that was in '65. We were friends until just before he died. We worked Vegas a lot together, at the same time. He came to see me at The Flamingo in 1968, because he said he wanted to make a comeback, live, because he hadn't sung live for years."

Priscilla Presley once said of this period: "You know, I think Elvis lost sight of his purpose in life, believe it or not.

He never really understood why all the adoration. He never really understood where, I think, he wanted to go. I know he wanted to be a great actor, but he honestly couldn't understand where it was all going. And he had to keep motivated and it was, you know, keeping him motivated, keeping him focused was very difficult… He loved to eat. He just, you know, he had a – that was probably one of our problems is that I don't have an addictive personality and living with someone who has an addictive personality was very, very difficult and very hard to watch. So it was a big issue."

At around this point Elvis began to become dependent on prescription drugs, although on which exact type is still uncertain. Johnny Cash recalled that Elvis always suffered from the rumours that constantly existed of his supposed drug habits: "Elvis certainly took a lot of abuse from that crowd. He had his problems with gossip, too, and rumour and lies. He was very sensitive, easily hurt by the stories people told about him being on dope and so on. I myself couldn't understand why people wanted to say that back in the 50s, because in those days he was the last person on earth who needed dope. He had such a high energy level that it seemed he never stopped – though maybe that's why they said he was on dope. Either way, he wasn't, or at least I never saw any evidence of it. I never saw him use any kind of drug, or even alcohol; he was always clear-headed around me, and very pleasant. Elvis was such a nice guy, and so talented and charismatic – he had it all – that some people just couldn't handle it and reacted with jealousy. It's only human, I suppose, but it's sad." He added: "He and I liked each other, but we weren't that tight – I was older than he was, for one thing, and married, for another – and we weren't close at all in his later years. I took the hint when he closed his world around him; I didn't try to invade his privacy. I'm so glad I didn't, either, because so many of his old friends were embarrassed so badly when they were turned away at Graceland. In the 60s and 70s he and I chatted on the phone a couple of times and swapped notes now and again. If he were closing at the Las Vegas Hilton as I was getting ready to open, he'd wish me luck, that kind of thing – but that was about the extent of it."

Wayne Jackson recalled to EWJ of the Vegas years: "When Elvis first opened at the International Hotel, we took the Learjet to Vegas… we would always get the table right in front. This would go on for six nights or seven nights in a row. After the show, we'd go back stage to the dressing room and hobnob with Elvis and the rest of the stars who were back there. That went on once or twice a year for several years. We also went to Elvis' house together, too. For a three or four year period, we went to Vegas, and at other times during the year, we'd go out to Graceland. The times we had fun were when we went to the movies late at night. We'd have a caravan of cars and we'd go to the Memphian. At 2 am we'd watch a movie or two. We went to the fairgrounds. That was a lot of fun. We were just a little group. Elvis would want to ride the Pippin and we'd all go ride the Pippin. When he was tired of that, we'd all go to the bumper cars and everybody would ride that. This was genuinely fun. People were loosened up much more there than at his house, where you were like in his environment. Those were really fun times. We would wait for him. I waited in that big old gnarly jungle chair in there, I sat in that thing, it swallowed me up. We'd get there, say, at 11 o'clock and he might not come downstairs 'til one. Whenever he felt like it he would finally come downstairs. Everybody was waiting and waiting and watching the staircase. By the time we were going to Vegas, Elvis was the superstar. He was the King then and he had taken the title for real, as opposed to 1969, when we did those sessions and Neil Diamond was the big star of the day. Everybody's opinion of their time around him kinda changed… What we always did was fool around in the kitchen for a little while and walk around drinking Cokes. There was usually a good crowd, 15 or 20 people maybe. They would line the cars up into a caravan at four, five or six in the morning to go out, maybe to the movies. When the movies were over and it was time to go back to Elvis' house, I would always beg out. I'd have to be back in the studio at noon or something, so I would beg off and go home and not go back to his house. I missed all that. Now, in retrospect, I wish I hadn't, but I was working, making records. I had to have three or four hours of sleep."

The legendary guitarist James Burton became a part of Elvis' band when the King took up residence in Vegas, as Burton recalled to journalist Arjan Deelen in 2001: "In 1969, Elvis called me. We talked for a long time. One of his opening lines was that he used to watch me play on Ricky Nelson's TV shows, and on Shindig. He said that he had followed my career for a long time. We talked about putting a band together. And when I first met him, it was like we had known each other our whole lives – background, music and everything. It was great. We did a rehearsal, and there was a drummer that I really admired, Richie Cross. During the break Richie came over to me and said: 'I really appreciate your call, and keeping me in mind to do this. But I don't think I want to do it. I don't want to work too hard!' So Larry Muhoberac got Ronnie Tutt to do the gig. Boy, he played so good."

Of the first night in Vegas, Burton recalled: "Elvis was very nervous about the opening. Of course, he'd been doing movies for nine years, and he felt that he was out of touch with the public. He was scared to death. Every critic and celebrity in the world was in the audience that night. Just before we went onstage, Elvis walked up to me backstage, and he said: 'James, I'm so nervous. I don't know if I can do this'. I said: 'Elvis,

don't worry about it. All you gotta do is walk out there'. And he said: 'I don't know, man. I'm so nervous I could climb the walls'. But I was right. When he walked out on that stage, it was just unbelievable. The audience was so loud, it sounded like a freight train. People were screaming, hollering. I don't think we heard anything the whole first show! Since I'd last seen him at the Hayride, he'd really matured into a great showman. He just had a way with the audience – he had a great communication with them. It was a very interesting situation."

Dates at the Houston Astrodome followed ("Yeah," Burton continued, "that was fantastic. It was really interesting how we were going to do this, because the place was so huge. God, there were so many people and they were so far away. And the sound. You'd hit a chord on the guitar, and four seconds later it would come back at you!") and sessions in Nashville: "Fender sent me a bunch of guitars, and there was one that was sort of special. It was solid rosewood. It was very heavy, and I didn't particularly care for the sound of it. But I played it, and Elvis said: 'Wow! That's a beautiful guitar'. I handed it to him, and he said: 'Whoa, this thing's heavy!' Fender first wanted me to have it, but I said no. Then they offered it to Elvis, who said: 'No, I have no use for it'. Then they tried to give it to Chip, but he wasn't interested either. But it was a good session. We had David Briggs, Jerry Carrigan, Chip Young, Charlie McCoy. Yeah, that was a great band. We had a great time."

He went on: "My main aim with Elvis was music, but we had a great communication. We did talk a lot. He would tell us different stories, things that happened when he was in the Army and stuff. If he wanted to talk to me, any given time, he'd just pick up the phone and call me. But my main thing with Elvis was the music… You had to watch him because he was a very good director. He might just decide to stop the song or something like that. The eye contact was very good. He sort of keyed off the guitar. He loved certain licks that I would play. If I would leave them out he'd miss it. Musically you had to know where he was at. You had to pay attention at all times. If you'd look away, you might lose your place in the show. It was interesting, because he never did the same thing twice."

By 1973 Elvis was looking for a new direction, as Burton related: "He went into an extreme musical change at that time. He wasn't really into any particular direction, so he was doing a lot of different stuff. Probably searching for something that he liked, fall into a different groove. He'd gotten to a point where he wanted to go back to small rhythm section stuff, rather than having a lot of strings and a lot of horns. He really wanted to make a change. At one time he would actually be into doing, like you say, a lot of blues. 'Big Boss Man' and 'Steamroller Blues', which he really loved. But sometimes he was also into gospel and country."

From then on Elvis slipped into a kind of semi-respectable, semi-ridiculous state of permanent residency in Vegas, wowing middle-aged crowds almost 20 years after his rock'n'roll glory days. Divorcing from Priscilla in 1973 (she had left him, unable to tolerate his slide into prescription drug addiction and gluttony) and squiring a succession of young women, it seemed that Elvis' days as a serious artist were over.

His lifestyle now overshadowed his musical career: for example, he had also developed something of an obsession with guns, amassing a collection of weapons and practising their use regularly. He once narrowly missed his girlfriend Linda Thompson with a bullet, as she told elvis.com.au: "He was just like a little child. It's astounding when you think about the guns that he had, because I'm so aware now of gun control and the danger of handguns. When I look back, and think about when he had guns around that were loaded and a young child around. You know, we just said to Lisa to never go near the guns, and she didn't. But who knows, if she had been a more disobedient child or a more curious child, it's astounding. It makes my blood run cold when I think about the responsibility... I'd just happened to have come out of the shower at the Las Vegas Hilton, the presidential suite, and he was lying on the sofa. In those days they had these huge bull's eye advertisements. Vegas came alive when Elvis was there, and they had these billboards, posters and placards. So he had one of these enormous bull's eye things in the suite and he decided that he would just shoot for the target. It was a kind of cardboard cutout of his name with this bull's eye... like hit the mark, come see Elvis... whatever. So, Elvis pulled out his gun and shot at the bull's eye and the bullet went through the wall, which was adjacent to my bathroom. It went through the wall, then through the toilet paper holder, which was metal, out through a mirrored door and shattered it. I was standing at the sink and I heard ting, ting, and the sound of glass breaking. I felt the air behind my leg. When I looked down there was a bullet hole in the door behind me. I opened that door and there was another shattered glass door and a bullet lying there... I threw my robe on, put a towel around my head and went outside and said, 'What do you think you're doing? You almost shot me!' and he went white. It was as though someone had told him that the bullet had gone through the wall and that I was hit. He couldn't even get up because he was so shaken... He said, 'Oh my God, I didn't know you were in there. I didn't know it would go through the wall. I thought it would just lodge there.' I said, 'You could have killed me!' and he asked if I wanted to go home. I said, 'Well, at least I won't get shot at there!' He was profusely apologetic, but he was really shaken up. He was ashen."

Despite his artistic and physical decline, few expected Elvis' early death in the summer of 1977: after an all-night session, he was discovered in his bathroom by his fiancée Ginger Alden.

He had apparently succumbed to a heart attack while seated on the lavatory.

The public, who had ignored him for so long, went into an orgy of emotion on his death. President Jimmy Carter said: "Elvis Presley's death deprives our country of a part of itself. He was unique and irreplaceable. His music and his personality, fusing the styles of white country and black rhythm and blues, permanently changed the face of American popular culture. His following was immense and he was a symbol to people the world over, of the vitality, rebelliousness, and good humour of his country." His body was eventually interred at Graceland and the Presley industry went into overdrive, launching a flood of merchandise and audio releases which continues to this day.

As Loanne Parker recalled: "The day that Elvis died, Colonel and his basic staff were in Portland waiting for Elvis to arrive. I was in my room. I was doing some work. And Colonel was in the room that usually we would have, he would have a suite, and we would use the living room area as a temporary office. He came to my room, knocked on the door and I could see he was physically upset. He said, 'They have some bad news'. He said, 'I've got a call and they think, they're not sure that Elvis is going to live.' He said, 'I'll keep you updated'. And he went back to his temporary office. And of course I was in shock. I remember I just paced the floor. I was in shock because honest to God we never thought Elvis would die. He had almost become bigger than life to us and he felt he could handle everything… suddenly to think that it would be gone was just inconceivable, you couldn't believe it. I felt it was going to be all right. And then, of course, Colonel came and he said, 'He's gone'."

Priscilla told Larry King: "I was at home – actually, I was on my way to an appointment… And Joe Esposito had gotten a hold of my parents and said that he needed to talk to me. They reached my sister and my sister met me at the appointment and told me that something was wrong, that Elvis was ill and in the hospital and I went back home. The phone was ringing and it was Joe on the phone who said that he was sending a plane for me to come to Memphis. It was serious… He said it was serious and that Elvis died… His father, right, was in such a state of shock. I mean, I can still hear him to this day, you know, wailing. It was – he honestly couldn't handle anything. Everyone was in disarray, the whole household… My daughter? Surprisingly enough, I don't think she really knew the impact nor did she really know what had happened. And it was very difficult for her to believe. I remember that she was – she took a golf cart that she would ride around Graceland in, and she was out with her friend. And I thought that was a little odd, but then again, remembering the age. And I actually preferred her to be out than in the house because it was very depressing."

Of the end of Elvis' career, James Burton recalled: "Elvis gained weight, but he loved food and he had that little Southern boy habit of eating Southern fried food. And he loved ice cream. Big balls of ice cream. Something I noticed is that he'd gain a lot of weight, and then he'd go on an extreme diet and lose a lot of weight real fast. But his death came as a great shock. I had no idea… We were in a plane flying to Portland, Maine, to play a show on August 17th. The band was flying down on the 16th, and during the flight we were asked to return to Las Vegas. We all wondered why we were going back. I knew that his dad Vernon had had some heart problems, and I wondered if something had happened to Vernon. We had no idea why Elvis would cancel the tour. We landed in San Pablo, Colorado to refuel. Marty Harrel, the trombone player, said he'd call Vegas to hear what was going on. Marty was coming back, came up to me and put his arm around me, and said: 'Elvis has passed away'. Cold chills went over me, I just couldn't believe it. I said: 'Is this a joke?' 'No, it's for real', he said. We had to walk back and tell the other members. Boy, it was a long flight back to Vegas. It was just an incredibly sad time. An incredible loss for the entire world and the music industry… I miss him. I love his music, I loved him as a person. I will always think of him as one of the greatest entertainers of all time. He'll be terribly missed."

Wayne Jackson said: 'The day he died I had just flown back into Nashville and pulled up to a Ruby Tuesday. I went in and when the people that I knew from the music business saw me, they jumped up and ran over and pulled me outside, out the front door! I said, 'What in the world is going on?' They said, 'Haven't you heard, don't you know?' 'No, I don't know.' 'Well sit down.' they said, as though I were a family member or something. They told me Elvis had died. I was moving to Nashville from Memphis myself when I learned Elvis was dead.

I thought, 'Well, I'm the last holdout. That's one more thing that is over with for good.' Stax was gone. American was gone. Hi was gone. Al Green wasn't making pop records anymore. Steve Cropper had left town. Reggie and Bobby Wood and Bobby Emmons, Chips Moman, all the people from American had left town and I was the last one. They could have turned the lights out. It was all over. Elvis was dead. Otis was dead. It was just over. I was the last guy leaving Memphis. I thought, 'What a shame. This is really the end of this era.' The man who brought it all into focus and made the world catch on fire with rock'n'roll was Elvis Presley. He also generated those fires in me and my friends. We all thought we could be like him. Some of us, like me, were lucky enough to get a little piece of that flame. I've had a good life with music. I enjoy it and have a little special feeling for what I do. You can't learn how to do that."

After Elvis' death, Vernon's second wife Dee – Elvis' stepmother – wrote a sensational book in which she claimed that Elvis committed suicide, among other generally disregarded claims. Esposito countered: "Towards the end of his life, Elvis may have been self-destructive by taking all those drugs. But no way did he consciously end his own life. I was constantly with Elvis during the last months. Sure he was fascinated by the afterlife, and he did talk about what it may be like in the spiritual world... But Elvis loved life. He lived to perform on stage. The night before he died, he was planning a concert tour. Dee Presley was no longer living in Memphis at the time. All her claims are lies and based on hearsay... Those terrible claims are coming from a very bitter and angry old woman. I wonder if she is getting back at Vernon, because he wrote her out of his will. Vernon left her nothing! Now I can understand why Elvis was always sceptical of Dee, and why Elvis did not attend their wedding... Of all the fabricated stories to have emerged since Elvis died, this book is the worst – ever! I'm shocked!...

I hope and pray that Graceland and Priscilla Presley will make an official statement to the press to discredit Dee and her ugly book. Personally, I would like to see Priscilla take Dee Presley to court for defamation. Maybe that will stop other people from writing such obscene stories about Elvis in the future."

As Priscilla told Larry King in 2003, "He was wonderfully loving. Caring… But he was also a victim of his own career, of his own love, which of course was music, and going into film. He was a product of the business. And that was his only way of life. He loved it. He, you know, he travelled all over before he was even really discovered by Colonel Parker. And had venues that he would appear at… I had probably an illusion of being the wife that, you know, I wanted to create a home. I wanted to have children. I wanted him to be a husband. It was never going to be that way. It couldn't be that way. He had created a lifestyle that was really very necessary for him because he couldn't get around without fanfare… As a person, he was wonderful. He really was a great person. He was full of life. He had a great sense of humour. Very talented, of course, but very caring to his parents. There was a very endearing quality about Elvis."

The actress Linda Thompson, another one of Elvis' girlfriends, told elvis.com.au of their first meeting: "It was the middle of July in Memphis and it was very humid, just sweltering. He had on this black cape with a high collar and a red satin lining, and I said 'Dressed a little like Dracula, aren't we?', so you see, we both shared a sense of humour that was very much like the other. We just hit it off immediately because we grew up in Memphis, we had the same religious beliefs, the same love for our family, devotion to mother and father. We had the same sense of loyalty, we enjoyed the same cuisine because we were both Southerners… We talked about marriage often. We talked about having children too. When Elvis was in the hospital a couple of times with pneumonia and other health problems, I stayed in the hospital with him for two and a half weeks at a time. I had my own hospital bed that was pushed up against his. I even ate hospital food. I was a young, healthy, vibrant girl but I'm in a hospital bed pressing the buttons to move up and down in tandem with him. The TV shows would go off at night, we didn't have all-night cable like we do now, and we'd turn the monitor to the nursery and pick out the different babies that we'd like to have… he died only eight months after I left. We did speak once or twice because I worried about him and I would call. I called Graceland a couple of times just to see how he was because I was worried."

Perhaps Elvis might have roused himself from his condition and survived, given the right circumstances. One rather unusual member of Elvis' entourage was Larry Geller, hired as his personal hairdresser in 1964 and evolving over time to the status of spiritual guru, lending Elvis a vast library of books on the occult and supernatural philosophy. After Elvis' death Geller wrote several books on his time with Presley, telling Elvis

Presley News: "Little did I suspect [one] afternoon in April of 1977, in Elvis' suite at the Hilton Hotel in Detroit while we were on tour, where our conversation would eventually lead. Briefly and to the point, while we were talking in his bedroom, Elvis became very serious, he spoke of his nagging health problems: his spastic colon, glaucoma, hypertension, insomnia, sore throats and his fluid retention and bloated condition. He was fully [aware] of all the pills and prescription drugs he was taking, and his unhealthy eating habits. He actually said that it was a miracle he was still in one piece. Elvis was very concerned how the fans might be judging his appearance and he expressed in no uncertain terms his desire and definite plans to change his lifestyle and career."

He went on: "Then Elvis put his hands on my shoulders, looked squarely in my eyes, and with his typical sense of drama declared that we had a 'special' task together. He asked for my help, and said he wouldn't ask anyone else. He said he needed to

know if I was behind him in this… that otherwise his real story and the truth of his life would never be known. Elvis spoke of writing a book; he wanted to call it Through My Eyes, hoping to offset and balance what he knew others were planning at that time. Elvis felt that his image was what most people related to, and he really desired that his fans and the general public learn more about his inner life, his values and what he was aspiring toward. After further discussion I promised him I would help him write his book, and 'tell the world the truth'. We shook hands and hugged to seal our mutual vow. Looking back, I really feel that even if Elvis hadn't asked me, I probably would have written a book anyway. I have a lot to say and I'm very passionate about it."

David Stanley, who had grown up in Elvis' shadow as his stepbrother, said: "I think the interesting thing about Elvis, being around him all the years I was, and I think all the guys can relate to this, was watching Elvis be Elvis… When people talk about him and how big he is… he was such a magnet, people were just drawn to him. He had a hard time being that. I mean, he was being Elvis Presley. I think in the end that's what caught up with him. How do you become a person that everybody loves? How do you become a person everybody adores and follows and wants to be around and wants that pat on the back? Watching him being Elvis, cool Elvis, up Elvis, down Elvis, sad Elvis, the great entertainer he was, watching him do that and towards the end, watching him go through that. Many times he would sit down by himself and say, why me? Why I do have these phenomenal gifts? He always wanted to share it but he always had that problem of, why has this been bestowed on me… Elvis loved to love people but it was difficult for letting people love him or us love him. He would just go inside himself and try to figure out who we was."

Waylon Jennings had a view on the Memphis Mafia, saying:

"Red West may have been one of the best friends he ever had, and Sonny West, because they cared about him, watched over him, trying to keep him alive. Elvis may have been the most beautiful man in the world. His face was carved like a stone, chiselled out of rock, he was just that good looking, and his voice was unbelievable. He was a phenomenon, and he arrived fully formed. From the first notes of 'That's All Right Mama', as otherworldly as they were, he never improved, or even developed. He hardly changed from start to finish, and Colonel Parker didn't help. I think a monkey could have managed Elvis, and maybe done a better job. Colonel Tom wanted to manage me once but said I was uncontrollable. He was probably right."

Larry Geller later told Fryman: "Oh, if only he had taken care of himself as well as he took care of others. If he did he would probably be here with us today. He ate the unhealthiest food, and broke all the nutritional laws. He was for many years in denial of his pill addiction that only grew worse until his body bore the full brunt, as he really began to suffer, and eventually pay the ultimate price. It wasn't as if Elvis was in the dark, and didn't know the facts. He was aware, he read a variety of nutritional books I brought him over the years, from many of the leading health authorities. We had many discussions about diet and health. He had a doctor's manual listing all the drugs and their horrible side effects, and he read it. But there were many forces at work, pulling him down. First and foremost was his dependency, and the overwhelming fact of being Elvis – superman – and his public image. You have to remember these were the days before celebrities went public concerning their substance abuse. These were the days before the Betty Ford Clinic, and there weren't many places to go for help, let alone the aspect of disgrace and embarrassment."

In 1981 the American journalist Albert Goldman wrote a scurrilous biography entitled Elvis, which shocked many fans with its graphic discussion of Presley's supposedly aberrant sexual, dietary, narcotic and even toiletry habits. Among its many claims was a suggestion that Red West had had a relationship with Priscilla, to which the former bodyguard replied: "I did take an issue with Albert Goldman's book. I would never have given him an interview if I had known where he was going with it. I was told by him that he was doing an in-depth book on Elvis, but nothing crossed my mind he was going to write such a terrible book that could not be justified in my mind. I did the interview because Lamar [Fike, another member of the Memphis Mafia] asked me to do it for him. When I first heard about the negativity in the book, I grabbed the book that Albert Goldman had sent me, but I had not read it... I looked up in the reference file of the book and looked at the pages where my name was mentioned or where I was saying something. My interview with him was based on the agreement that I would speak only on the subjects I wished to talk about, and he was not to imply that I said something that I didn't say, or include me in something that I didn't do. After looking up my name on each page that was listed in the reference list, I didn't find anything that indicated he violated that agreement with me. But I don't remember coming across anything related to me and Priscilla having any kind of relationship, other than she was Elvis' wife and I treated her with respect as such."

Colonel Parker died in 1997, outliving his client by a full two decades. Although he has been painted as a scheming, exploiting manager of the worst sort, it seems that he had his gentle side. As Loanne Parker said, "He played Santa Claus for the children at the Christmas parties. We could be driving, or going to dinner, and he would say to me, 'Stop, pull over'. He would see someone who was standing on the street that he knew needed something. And he'd get out of the car and go over and give them five dollars, ten dollars, twenty dollars, whatever he felt they needed. Many times we'd be eating in the restaurant and he'd see an old couple eating a very meagre meal. And he would call the waitress over and say, 'Tell those people I'd like to buy their dinner'. Maybe they could order a little more. He was always doing things like that. He gave hundreds and thousands of dollars to charities. Always with the stipulation, no publicity."

After Elvis' death, Priscilla went on to become a successful actress and charity campaigner. Her daughter Lisa-Marie's fate was rather more complex: in predictable style she endured drug abuse and a lack of direction before establishing a reasonably successful music career. However, a brief marriage to Michael Jackson almost sank her credibility before she really got started. As she told Playboy, "I knew there was going to be more attention on me that anyone else putting out a debut record. If I wanted to be a novelty, I could have easily called a top writer and turned into a pop star. I could have done that years ago. But I wanted to be looked at as an artist, so I couldn't do anything stupid or shallow or silly… I don't like talking about myself. At this point I'm thinking, what have I done? The hard part is opening up for the first time. I have to combat 30 years of speculation and tabloid stuff. I have to go out there and say, 'Hi, I'm not that person'. However, I understand the curiosity… People get all kinds of crazy ideas to turn me into a goofball. A whole record of Elvis covers and duets. We can put you in a white suit! Sorry, Britney already took the cake on that one." Asked if she found her heritage a help or a hindrance, she added: "It's only a hindrance in that I didn't ask for all the attention, so I have a phobia against it. I don't ask tabloids to chase me around every week. But at the same time, I would never take back any part of who I am or where I came from. I would never want to be part of anything else. I'm honored and proud of my family and my dad… it helped me get a foot in the door. But you have to hold your own. And again, it's a hindrance, because a lot of attention and pressure is on me. It's a little scary… The back lawn of Graceland is a graveyard, basically. How many people have a family grave in the backyard? How many people are reminded of their fate, their mortality, every day? All the graves are lined up and there's a spot there, waiting for me, right next to my grandmother."

Lisa Marie added of her father's work: "I like the 70s material because I was around for those recordings. There was some great stuff that never made it to the radio: a song called 'Mary in the Morning', which I loved. 'In The Ghetto'. I like the darker songs, the sad ones. There's a song called 'Separate

Ways' that was treacherously painful. And 'How Great Thou Art', when he'd sing that live, there was nothing like it. I'd go to his shows, and he was awesome... When they divorced, I would go out on the road more and miss more school, which I liked. People say I didn't get to see him very much, but I was with him quite a bit. All of a sudden, a car would show up at school, and he was calling for me to go out on the road... It was always a lot of fun. There is not one bad memory. There was always a lot of energy and life in the house. He was very mischievous... I don't feel like I was spoiled. Anything my father did for me or gave me was done out of love, and I took it as that. I'm sure I had moments when I was a snot. But my mom was there to smack me back to the other side. Whatever he did, she cleaned up."

In 2001 James Burton and others returned to live arenas with the improbable spectacle of Elvis The Concert, a live show presided over by live footage of Elvis on an enormous screen.

Despite the unusual, not to say slightly macabre, nature of the performance, audiences loved it. As Burton explained: "The beauty of it is that it's very, very high class. If Elvis was here I don't think he would make any changes. He would love it, and I think he would be very honoured that we're doing it for him and his wonderful fans around the world. As long as the fans want it, and it's financially able to take care of itself, I think it would be very good to continue."

The late Johnny Cash summed it up well when he wrote in his autobiography: "I've heard it said that here at the end of the century, we all have our own Elvis, and I can appreciate that idea, even though my Elvis was my friend, flesh and blood in real life. Certainly, though, my Elvis was the Elvis of the 50s. He was a kid when I worked with him. He was 19 years old, and he loved cheeseburgers, girls, and his mother, not necessarily in that order (it was more like his mother, then girls, then cheeseburgers). Personally, I liked cheeseburgers and I had nothing against his mother, but the girls were the thing. He had so many girls after him that whenever he was working with us, there were always plenty left over. We had a lot of fun. We had a lot of fun in general, not just with the girls. It was nice that we could make a living at it, but every one of us would have done it for free. And you know, Elvis was so good. Every show I did with him, I never missed the chance to stand in the wings and watch. We all did. He was that charismatic."

As Wayne Jackson recalled to EWJ: "Elvis Presley took off when I was 10 years old. He was on the radio and I was close enough to feel the heat at a real impressionable age. I think all of us that lived here and knew about him and later, maybe met him, were touched by the thought that it could be us. You don't ever know when that might happen to a person. I know I was inspired to be in a little band and stay in the music business. If it had been before Elvis, I maybe wouldn't have done it. So, I think he inspired everybody in the city that was close enough to hear the blast."

He added, of the cultural impact of Elvis' work: "The black people, I sincerely believe, respect his success. If they don't respect what he sang, they respect his success. You have to. Now that his career is over, when you look back at what the great songs were that he sang, he was a truly great singer. He was a great gospel singer because he loved it. But at that particular moment in 1969, because of those films he was in and all the little light flimsy songs he was singing, he wasn't held in high regard by us except for the fact that he was in the movies. That wasn't as impressive as Neil Diamond. But, he took off again and was truly his splendid self. Elvis was the greatest singer in the world but even he couldn't make 'Suspicious Minds' out of 'Teddy Bear'. The same thing with the movies. Elvis is really being Elvis in those movies no matter what his clothes or his name is. I admire him for it. I like that. I wish he'd have gotten a good part. I wish he'd have gotten to prove himself just one time. He could have if he'd have been here long enough. One day someone would have let him play a legitimate role."

The statistics that have emerged since then about his unique career are staggering. He became one of a mere four artists to have two albums in the US Top 5 at the same time, alongside rapper Nelly, his contemporary Roy Orbison and 80s metal upstarts Guns N' Roses. He entered the Rock And Roll Hall of Fame in 1986, the Country Music Hall of Fame in 1998 and the Gospel Music Hall of Fame in 2001. In 2005 Forbes magazine stated that – for five years in a row – Elvis was the dead artist who earned the most money: his estate grossed $45 million that year.

Although much of Presley's legacy is tainted by the aroma of kitsch and irony, propagated by the many Elvis impersonators in jumpsuits that plague the world's nightspots, real connoisseurs know how important his early work was. This was reinforced in 2002 when a remix of his little-known soundtrack song 'A Little Less Conversation' was given a strangely outdated big-beat reworking by the DJ Junkie XL and used by Nike in their commercials in the run-up to the World Cup football tournament of that year. It made No. 1 in several countries, as did a simultaneous greatest-hits compilation called Elv1s: 30.

The song was huge, even if Junkie XL's name was changed at the request of the Elvis estate to JXL: as the DJ said, "[the name JXL] was used only once for the Elvis remix, which was a request of the Elvis family. They thought 'Junkie' was too much, connected with Elvis, even though he was known to be the biggest junkie on the planet, but anyway. I thought it was funny, pure one hundred percent proper English humour. But unfortunately that didn't make it to the US. So it was once JXL and now it just gets used like vice versa, especially for things like posters, where JXL might come across more powerfully than Junkie XL. That's how people make decisions now, but my real artist name is Junkie XL and sometimes JXL is just a shortcut." Of the song, he said: "It was done for a Nike commercial. When the commercial aired, the music took over the commercial and it started living its own life."

The following year Paul Oakenfold's remix of 'Rubberneckin' followed in the footsteps of 'A Little Less Conversation', both in style and commercial success. In 2004, a fiftieth-anniversary release of his first song, 'That's All Right Mama' was an international hit. Amazingly, his posthumous career didn't stop there, with RCA issuing 18 singles of his chart-topping hits, one per week, in a collector's box.

And so the incredible tale of the most famous entertainer in history continues to this day. If his legions of fans are to be entrusted with his legacy, it's a fair prediction to say that Elvis will never die.

TRACK-BY-TRACK ANALYSIS

This song-by-song run-through of Elvis Presley's recorded catalogue seeks to provide a clear, unbiased assessment of each of his albums from 1956 to 1963, as well as a last-ditch attempt from 1977. While some of the material he released in the 60s and 70s was original (not a soundtrack and not a compilation) and a small percentage of this was reasonably good, I've decided to keep the focus positive here and concentrate on his period of greatest quality. I've given each song a rating out of five as follows:

★ ★ ★ ★ ★ Absolutely essential
★ ★ ★ ★ Excellent
★ ★ ★ Average
★ ★ Poor
★ Terrible

Elvis Presley
(1956)

Tracklisting: Blue Suede Shoes / I'm Counting On You / I Got A Woman / One-Sided Love Affair / I Love You Because / Just Because / Blue Moon / Trying To Get To You / I'm Gonna Sit Right Down and Cry (Over You) / I'll Never Let You Go (Little Darlin') / Tutti Frutti / Money Honey

Blue Suede Shoes ★ ★ ★ ★ ★
"Well, it's one for the money / Two for the show / Three to get

ready / Now go, cat, go ...." What a way to open your debut album, and unsurpassed as a signal of intent. Carl Perkins' original had been a groundbreaking fusion of blues, country and pop, but Presley's version – recorded just two months later – makes that seem positively pedestrian in comparison. A raucous rhythmic attack, drums prominent in the mix, a sloppy guitar solo by Scotty Moore, and a frenetic Elvis vocal: put those ingredients together and you have bona fide classic destined for a place in the rock'n'roll pantheon.

I'm Counting On You ★ ★ ★
With the piano lines of Floyd Cramer to the fore, 'I'm Counting On You' is a country-tinged ballad, which is thought to have been suggested to Elvis by Steve Sholes. It's a beautifully accomplished treatment of the ballad by Don Robertson – and the record company's attempt to demonstrate that there was more to Elvis than just the incendiary teenage rebellion of 'Blue Suede Shoes' et al.

I Got A Woman ★ ★ ★
Unlike his white contemporaries (step forward, Pat Boone) Elvis did not attempt to sweeten his interpretations of the R&B hits of the day. His take on 'I Got A Woman' by Ray Charles, a song that still sounds fresh today thanks to Kanye West – improves on the orchestrated original by pushing the guitars to the forefront, and is blessed by a passionate vocal from Presley. An early staple of the Elvis live set, the modern rock'n'roll as we know it starts here.

One-Sided Love Affair ★ ★ ★ ★
'One-Sided Love Affair' – a Steve Sholes rather than an Elvis choice – is another country-tinged song, but this time fortified with rock'n'roll power. All of the soon-to-be trademark Presley vocal mannerisms and inflections are present and correct. In a playful mood, he even imitates the Buddy Holly hiccup

and manages to send up any romantic tension in the lyrics by Bill Campbell. The good-natured honky-tonk piano and the distinctive one-note piano solo all contribute to a delightful sense of the absurd. Elvis might not be for "no one-sided love affair", but the curl in his voice let's you know that the girl is won over in the end.

I Love You Because ★ ★ ★ ★

The first of five Sun recordings lifted for inclusion for Elvis Presley's debut on RCA, 'I Love You Because' is another ballad that demonstrates the purity and gentle caress of that voice. If the producers of this album did one thing right, it was to recognise his vocal qualities and push the Elvis voice high up in the mix. This one set its stall out to make the teenage girls swoon and succeeds.

Just Because ★ ★ ★ ★

Nothing syrupy on view in this song: 'Just Because' is carried along by anger, with Elvis trying to put a woman in her place with mean-spirited jabs. He's been dumped and it hurts. And this number conveys a delicious sense of spite and bite, like on the lines, "Well, well, well / Just because you think you're so pretty / And just because your momma thinks you're hot" – ouch, beware an Elvis scorned.

Blue Moon ★ ★ ★ ★

Elvis croons over an atmospheric clip-clop backing on this standard by Rodgers & Hart. Later covered by the mighty Bob Dylan on Self Portrait, the song is a true American classic, like a drifter on a dusty, desolate highway.

Trying To Get To You ★ ★ ★ ★

On top form, and sounding confident, the young Elvis produces a rousing vocal about his girl's love letter. His father's favourite and a song that he would turn to throughout his career – in particular during the 1970s. Listen and you will understand why.

I'm Gonna Sit Right Down and Cry (Over You) ★ ★ ★ ★

Elvis paying tribute to one of his heroes, Roy Hamilton, on 'I'm Gonna Sit Right Down and Cry (Over You)', which bears some comparison with its predecessor 'Trying To Get To You'. This time, the blues is replaced with rock'n'roll attack and very effective it is too.

I'll Never Let You Go (Little Darlin') ★ ★ ★ ★

Strange! Bit of an unremarkable aural drifter until a sudden change of tempo and speed nearly two minutes in, which gives the listener an appreciation of what all the fuss was about. This one leaves you with a shocked expression like an unexpected fright in the dark.

Tutti Frutti ★ ★ ★

Here, Elvis does his best to breathe new energy into the classic Little Richard song. There's nothing wrong with Presley's vocal technique, which handles the falsetto cries with ease, but the result is a treatment that is too polished and the raw excitement generated by Little Richard's gruff delivery is missing. He would do better later on with 'Jailhouse Rock' and 'Hound Dog'. Not even the great Elvis can pull off, "Womp-bomp-a-loom-op-a-womp-bam-boom!" with the same gusto as Little Richard.

Money Honey ★ ★ ★ ★

"You need money honey / if you want to get along with me ..." sings Elvis on his treatment of the minor hit for The Drifters in 1953. The sound of a band on a roll after 'Heartbreak Hotel', on this number – penned by Jesse Stone of 'Shake, Rattle and Roll' fame – Elvis is clearly at the top of his game. Gene Vincent obviously paid attention, as it bears a remarkable resemblance to the melody of 'Be Bop A Lula'.

Elvis Presley No. 2
(1956)

Tracklisting: Rip It Up / Love Me / When My Blue Moon Turns To Gold Again / Long Tall Sally / Paralysed / First In Line / So Glad Your Mine / Old Shep / Reddy Teddy / Anyplace Is Paradise / How's The World Treating You / How Do You Think I Feel

Rip It Up ★ ★ ★
"I'm gonna rip it up / And ball tonight" – another immortal rock'n'roll line – and this time it's Presley in another homage to the great Little Richard. The 'Saturday night and you just got paid' feeling is a joy that's universal. But, again, you have to say that the rasping Little Richard vocal on the original is difficult to beat. Still, it's miles better than the version by Bill Haley.

Love Me ★ ★ ★ ★
With a straight vocal delivery, Elvis saves this song from the parody country-and-western song that was the original intention of Lieber & Stoller (of 'Yakety Yak' fame). Presley excels himself here and gives a vocal performance of great sincerity that puts this song up there with some of his greatest ballads. It was the melodrama that made the girls swoon.

When My Blue Moon Turns To Gold Again ★ ★ ★ ★
You can tell that 'When My Blue Moon Turns To Gold Again' was one of the King's favourite country standards. One of the standout tracks on this album with a relaxed, confident vocalisation from Mr P.

Long Tall Sally ★ ★ ★
Another Little Richard song that has been covered many times through the years. However, it would be the Elvis template

that carried the biggest influence, as in faraway England and in distant Liverpool, the four men who would become the lovable moptops were listening and taking notes...

Paralysed ★ ★ ★ ★
Clearly, this song was a pleasure to record as you can hear the sheer joy in Presley's vocal. And all the while, he is supported by 'ba, ba, ba' backing vocals, which sound a bit daft, but they nevertheless, together with the powerful drumming, make this tune a hugely enjoyable listening experience.

First In Line ★ ★ ★ ★
A slightly muddy production notwithstanding, it's a decent number and on this track Elvis shows what set him apart from the other rock'n'rollers in the same era. Elvis you were, indeed, the 'first in line'.

Old Shep ★ ★ ★
One rocker and his dog, 'Old Shep' is another big beautiful country ballad – originally by Red Foley – and with its celestial backing it's guaranteed to make you feel a bit emotional. Sentimental, yes, but it's a real Elvis tear-jerker.

Reddy Teddy ★ ★ ★ ★
'The Boy Can't Help It': it's another cover of a Little Richard hit record. As with the other Little Richard tracks on this album, and with 'Tutti Frutti' before that, it rocks, but not as hard as Mr Richard Fenniman does. Mind you, Elvis begat Cliff Richard and Marty Wilde and this tune was a much revered favourite of the UK rock'n'rollers.

Anyplace Is Paradise ★ ★ ★
Yes, "Anyplace is paradise / When I'm with you" croons Elvis. Well, yes – it's a decent performance of a good song, slightly diminished, however, by the fogginess of the production.

How's The World Treating You? ★ ★ ★

Another country ballad, 'How's The World Treating You' is another composition with that rich voice to the fore. Although it doesn't stray into quite the same emotional territory as 'Old Shep', it's still a good song by most people's standards – although not inspirational.

How Do You Think I Feel ★ ★ ★ ★

This is a rockabilly inflected number, which finds Elvis Presley and his backing band on suitably impressive form and producing a little pearler, which has all the instinctive feel and energy of an artist at the top of his game. How Do You Think I Feel? Pretty damn good, actually.

Loving You
(1957)

Tracklisting: Mean Woman Blues / (Let Me Be Your) Teddy Bear / Loving You / Got A Lot O' Livin To Do! / Lonesome Cowboy / Hot Dog / Party / Blueberry Hill / True Love / Don't Leave Me Now / Have I Told You Lately That I Love You / I Need You So / Tell Me Why / Is It So Strange / One Night of Sin / When It Rains, It Really Pours / I Beg of You

Mean Woman Blues ★ ★ ★ ★

A prime slice of raw rock'n'roll, 'Mean Woman Blues' – a song later adapted successfully by the Big O – could easily pass for one of Elvis's legendary Sun recordings. The lyrics – "I got a woman / Mean as she can be" and "Sometimes I think / She's almost mean as me" – are rendered with Presley's usual swagger and, on this excellent track, he is ably supported by some wonderful doo-wah backing.

(Let Me Be Your) Teddy Bear ★ ★ ★ ★ ★
On the jaunty, highly catchy 'Teddy Bear' by Bernie Lowe and Kal Man, the Colonel's boy comes on all submissive for the girl of his dreams. "Put a chain around my neck and lead me anywhere / Oh let me be (oh let him be) / Your teddy bear", sings Elvis the Pelvis in that instantly recognisable croon, which has been parodied many times (see 'Death Cab For Cutie' by the Bonzos), but never bettered.

Loving You ★ ★ ★
Elvis the schmaltzy crooner on the album title track, 'Loving You'. Backed by a simple piano motif and gently strummed guitar, Elvis comes on all syrupy and mushy for the one he loves. He declares, "There is only one for me, and you know who / You know that I'll always be loving you". An effective, albeit saccharine, rocker.

Got A Lot O' Livin To Do! ★ ★ ★ ★
An out and out rocker, Presley truly delivers on the electric guitar-driven 'Got A Lot O' Livin To Do' – as Elvis declares that "time's a wasting" and there is "a whole lot o' loving to do". When Elvis cries, "Come on baby" he sounds uncannily like Jerry Lee Lewis. All the while, the drums provide an effective counterpoint on the chorus making for one of the better rock'n'roll performances on this album.

Lonesome Cowboy ★ ★ ★ ★
'Lonesome Cowboy' is one of the King's more unusual and heartfelt songs. With its shuffling start and dramatic feel, he moves into Sons of the Pioneers territory and the listener is reminded, in particular, of their rendition of 'Blue Prairie'. It's a hauntingly beautiful Western ballad.

Hot Dog ★ ★
Pleasing and up-tempo, but nevertheless a bit of a throwaway

rock'n'roller, unfortunately. At 76 seconds it's Elvis filler, not killer.

Party ★ ★
You can't knock the sentiment of the line, "Let's have a party tonight" or (for that matter) the strangeness of "shaking a chicken in the middle of the room". In the end, though, this is a bit of a throwaway swinging rocker by numbers that, in the end, doesn't really satisfy the soul on repeated listens.

Blueberry Hill ★ ★ ★
Presley doesn't do too badly with his rendition of 'Blueberry Hill' – the song made legendary by Fats Domino. In inspired form (Domino was one the many artists that Elvis respected and admired) there is a moodiness and richness in his voice, none better than when he utters the words, "Love's sweet melody".

True Love ★ ★ ★
Elvis Presley shows he is up to the task of Cole Porter's tale of "Suntanned / windblown / honeymooners at last alone" on the ballad 'True Love'. His range and control is spot on, as he handles this song with credibility and sensitivity.

Don't Leave Me Now ★ ★ ★
The fact that 'Don't Leave Me Now' failed to impress Elvis – he later re-recorded it for Jailhouse Rock – doesn't mean that this track is not up to scratch. The performance, although Elvis felt that his vocals had been drowned out by The Jordanaires, is certainly up to scratch.

Have I Told You Lately That I Love You ★ ★
Here the King goes pop and, although there is much to be admired, it ends up sounding a bit safe and never threatens to catch fire. Nothing wrong with Presley's performance, but it doesn't sound dangerous enough, only strangely contained.

I Need You So ★ ★ ★ ★
On Ivory Joe Hunter's 'I Need You So', we find an emotional Elvis really putting his vocal capacity to test. His performance here really oozes passion and class.

Tell Me Why ★ ★ ★ ★
Another Elvis Presley vocals showcase, as he excels again on 'Tell Me Why'.

One Night Of Sin ★ ★ ★ ★
All the standard bluesy components file in for registration, as 'One Night Of Sin' is all stabbed piano and swishes of the drum cymbal. What we receive in abundance here is an impassioned and brilliant ballad singing performance from the man in the gold lamé suit.

When It Rains, It Really Pours ★ ★ ★ ★ ★
The other standout track – 'When It Rains, It Really Pours' – boasts one of Presley's most passionate blues performances, together with some great bluesy guitar licks from the legendary Scotty Moore. When Elvis wails that "Only you and heaven knows / About my troubles, troubles, troubles", you can't help but share his pain.

I Beg Of You ★ ★ ★
A brittle-textured song full of yearning, Elvis places himself at the mercy of the girl of his dreams, as he pleads "Darling please please love me too", for his feelings to be reciprocated. He was the King, but he wasn't too proud to beg on this catchy number.

Elvis' Christmas Album
(1957)

Tracklisting: Santa Claus Is Back In Town / White Christmas / Here Comes Santa Claus (Right Down Santa Claus Lane) / I'll Be Home For Christmas / Blue Christmas / Santa Bring My Baby Back (To Me) / O Little Town Of Bethlehem / Silent Night / (There'll Be) Peace in the Valley (Me) / I Believe / Take My Hand, Precious Lord / It Is No Secret (What God Can Do)

Santa Claus Is Back In Town ★ ★ ★ ★ ★

"Christmas", "Christmas" go the backing vocals and it's a performance of monumental proportions from Elvis, as he really lays down the blues, with his voice sounding almost like the rasp of sandpaper. Songwriters Lieber & Stoller really excelled themselves here on this raucous and perfect album opener.

White Christmas ★ ★ ★ ★

Think Christmas and you think of Irving Berlin's 'White Christmas' rendered by the late, great Bing Crosby. Berlin, however, was known not to like Presley's Drifters-like take on his classic Christmas tune and even campaigned against it. This view is difficult to swallow, as Presley's version, with its lilting, rocking-horse backing, is warm and affectionate, rather like a brandy taken in front of a roaring log fire.

Here Comes Santa Claus (Right Down Santa Claus Lane) ★ ★ ★

A charming, bouncy song that conveys the childhood excitement of Christmas Eve, with the clock ticking, ever so slowly, to the present unwrapping on Christmas morning. Put on your biggest woolly jumper, crack open the egg nog and let your modern cynicism fade away.

I'll Be Home For Christmas ★ ★ ★

One for all the family, as the King sings of presents under the tree and mistletoe, which evokes the true spirit of the festive season – that feeling of being at home for Christmas. It would be a hard-hearted person that could knock the sentiment of this song.

Blue Christmas ★ ★ ★

The flipside of 'White Christmas' is when the "blue snowflakes start falling". It's hard not to be reminded of the affectionate tribute of 'It'll be Lonely This Christmas' by the tiger feet of Mud. 'Blue Christmas' is all gently picked guitar, angelic backing vocals and a rich, low-register delivery from Elvis.

Santa Bring My Baby Back (To Me) ★ ★ ★ ★

To coin a cliché, 'Santa Bring My Baby Back' is a real Christmas cracker and one of those quintessential Elvis 50s rockers that is guaranteed – even more so than the egg nog – to get even the most geriatric listener jumping around. Let's hope Santa gave Elvis the gift that he wanted, because this song twinkles like a star.

O Little Town Of Bethlehem ★ ★ ★

A return to more traditional fare, Elvis gives a perfectly pitched performance of this touching song about the birthplace of Jesus. It has a peaceful lullaby-like quality, featuring the organ of Dudley Brooks, which creates the perfect atmosphere for drifting off to sleep, and that, in this case, is meant as a compliment.

Silent Night ★ ★ ★ ★

Elvis croons a Christmas message of peace and goodwill to all his fans on this standard of Yuletide fare. Although it's the vocal style that has been parodied a million times by karaoke singers everywhere, you can't beat the sentiment that manages, just about, to steer away from any accusations of schmaltz.

I Believe ★ ★ ★

A pretty straightforward, gospel-flavoured take on the Frankie Laine pop spiritual, with the kind of affected vocal that P.J. Proby would later build a career on. Here, Elvis the spiritualist was on inspirational form.

Take My Hand, Precious Lord ★ ★ ★ ★

A change in tempo from the earlier Christmas raucousness, 'Take My Hand, Precious Lord' provides a spiritual showcase for Presley's sonorous vocal chords. Suitably backed by a fittingly reverential atmosphere and some nice organ touches in the solo performed by Dudley Brooks.

(There'll Be) Peace in The Valley (For Me) ★ ★ ★

"There will be peace in the valley for me / some day" is sung in an almost woozy fashion by Elvis in this solemn reading of the gospel track by Thomas A. Dorsey. This is sacred music and a song for the wee, small hours on Christmas Eve.

It Is No Secret (What God Can Do) ★ ★ ★ ★

Elvis, again on inspirational form, delivers a towering performance in this eulogy to the man in the skies. There are few better or more fitting tributes to the presence of God.

King Creole
(1958)

Tracklisting: King Creole / As Long As I Have You / Hard Headed Woman / Trouble / Dixieland Rock / Don't Ask Me Why / Lover Doll / Crawfish / Young Dreams / Steadfast, Loyal and True / New Orleans

King Creole ★ ★ ★ ★

'King Creole' is another iconoclastic tune from the king of

rock'n'roll. Written by the world-famous Leiber & Stoller songwriting team, it comes on with Elvis' clipped – almost conspiratorial – delivery, like a train running faster and faster down the track, until it bursts into the joyous exclamation of a chorus. It also features a brilliant guitar solo from Scotty Moore. Rock'n'roll perfection.

As Long As I Have You ★ ★ ★ ★
Out of the countless ballads Elvis recorded throughout his career, there can be few that rank alongside 'As Long As I Have You'. It is clear that Colonel Tom Parker's charge really enjoyed singing on this track, and this is passed onto the listener in spades.

Hard Headed Woman ★ ★ ★
Written by Claude Demetrius, 'Hard Headed Woman' moves with momentum, even though it has some strange sounding horns and weak backing vocals (not from the unimpeachable Jordanaires). This, plus the continual 'ha ha hoom' vocals from Elvis, make for one of his less interesting rockers.

Trouble ★ ★ ★ ★ ★
Without doubt one of the hardest rocking and aggressive Elvis performances of all time. 'Trouble' – which at times is reminiscent of Muddy Waters and Bo Diddley – is right up there with the very best of Elvis, and as an example of raw, full-on rock'n'roll, it can't be beaten. Would you dare argue with the line, "If you're looking for trouble / Just look right in my face"? Thought not… Little wonder that the King chose to revisit this song for his December '68 comeback.

Dixieland Rock ★ ★ ★
Another one from Demetrius, this time paired with Fred Wise, 'Dixieland Rock' comes close to hitting the spot. It begins with a momentum similar to 'Hard Headed Woman', but it struggles

to overcome the unwelcome, and all too obvious, Dixieland-style jazz horns.

Don't Ask Me Why ★ ★ ★
On the face of it, 'Don't Ask Me Why' is a standard ballad, with a by-now trademark quivering, affected vocal from Elvis. It does have some aural pleasures for the listener, the 'doo, doos' on the backing vocals after Elvis exhorts, "I want you so", and some customary simple piano touches.

Lover Doll ★ ★
"Lover doll, oh lover doll", repeats Elvis on this song (written by Sid Wayne with Abner Silver) that, if nothing else, has plenty of bounce to recommend it. Other lyrics such as, "You're the cutest lover doll / That I ever did see", confirm the tendency for this type of track to drag Elvis into a romantic swamp that he would find difficult to escape.

Crawfish ★ ★ ★ ★
Once heard, 'Crawfish' lingers long in the memory and it is another gem in the Elvis repertoire of great songs. Reaffirming his singing talents, 'Crawfish' has an unusual, funky rhythm embellished by a magnificent bluesy delivery from Presley. Certainly a whole lot better than his other dalliance into fish territory on 'Song of the Shrimp'.

Steadfast, Loyal and True ★ ★ ★
"We'll remember you / Dear alma mater / We're steadfast, loyal and true", the chorus lines of this school song (again by Lieber & Stoller) delivered with touching sensitivity by Elvis, which you have to say ain't bad for a trucker. So convincing was the song, it was later adopted by his own appreciation society.

New Orleans ★ ★ ★ ★
This is the blues with a capital B. 'New Orleans' is a stuttering and howling tour de force from the King of Creole. An

absolutely intuitive blues reading from the gutter, it deserves more recognition.

Elvis Is Back!
(1960)

Tracklisting: Make Me Know It / Fever / The Girl of My Best Friend / I Will Be Home Again / Dirty, Dirty Feeling / The Thrill of Your Love / Soldier Boy / Such a Night / It Feels So Right / Girl Next Door Went A' Walking / Like A Baby / Reconsider Baby

Make Me Know It ★ ★ ★ ★
After two years away in the Army, what a way to bounce back! 'Make Me Know It' is a pounding, gospel-flavoured rocker and one of the standout cuts to be recorded in the aftermath of the King's return from uniform.

Fever ★ ★ ★ ★
'Fever' will be forever synonymous with Peggy Lee, but Presley's take runs it close, as it provides the perfect vehicle for the King's deep vocal register. 'Fever' is the sound of Elvis in control, equal parts catlike, slinky and sexual. A simply majestic reading of this standard.

The Girl Of My Best Friend ★ ★ ★ ★
On the face of it, another teen ballad. Elvis is in love with the 'Girl Of My Best Friend', whom he describes with the usual platitudes like "a skin so fair". What sets it apart is the emotion that Elvis injects into this standard tale of unrequited love.

I Will Be Home Again ★ ★ ★
Presley sings, "I will be home again / Don't worry dear / I'll be home again" in this tune with some nice pop-styled dressing.

Dirty, Dirty Feeling ★ ★ ★ ★

As the title suggests, 'Dirty, Dirty Feeling' is a straight up and unashamed Nashville-styled rock'n'roller. If you want to chart an alternative history of Elvis – staying away from the obvious choices, 'Hound Dog' et al – then you could do worse than start here.

The Thrill Of Your Love ★ ★ ★ ★

This is a captivating and moving gospel-flavoured love ballad that strays comfortably into pop territory. Clearly, on this evidence, Elvis Aaron Presley stands for versatility.

Soldier Boy ★ ★ ★ ★

A superb doo-wop recording (perhaps the only one he ever did), 'Soldier Boy' showcases an Elvis determined not to be stereotyped as just another rock'n'roller. Presley succeeds here where others have failed.

Such a Night ★ ★ ★ ★

From one teen idol to another, this is a mighty fine reconstruction of the song made famous by Clyde McPhatter and the Drifters in R&B circles. As was par for the course, the Elvis version is much smoother, and he adroitly steers a course between knowing wit and innuendo.

It Feels So Right ★ ★ ★ ★

At the end of these slightly raunchy lines, "Step in these arms / Where you belong / It feels so right, so right", Elvis poses the question, "How can it be wrong?" Maybe Elvis, on his return from the army, was posing this question to all his fans. Yet another classic performance from the man who would be King.

Girl Next Door Went A' Walking ★ ★ ★

"The girl next door went a' walking / She found the boy she likes / She wanted to get married / Settle down for life" muses Elvis on this classy bit of pop-rock'n'roll with a 'doo-wah' backing. Jaunty, bouncy and upbeat, it's now a favourite fodder for all the karaoke all-stars out there.

Like A Baby ★ ★ ★ ★
This time, the theme is about a lover who cries like a baby because they can't break free of their deceitful partner. A bluesy saxophone part gives 'Like A Baby' some sparkle, and it ranks as a high point in the 'Presley sings the blues' canon. The accusatory tone of this Jesse Stone number fits Elvis like a glove.

Reconsider Baby ★ ★ ★ ★
A classic Presley blues interpretation, 'Reconsider Baby' deals with the universal topic of a love spurned. On the lines, "You said you once had loved me / But now I guess you've changed your mind", Elvis sounds committed, as he handles the bluesy vocal duties on this track with gusto and aplomb.

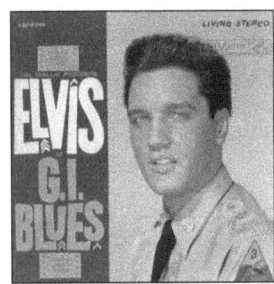

GI Blues
(1960)

Tracklisting: Tonight Is So Right For Love / What's She Really Like / Frankfort Special / Wooden Heart / Pocketful Of Rainbows / Shoppin' Around / Big Boots / Didja' Ever / Blue Suede Shoes / Doin' the Best I Can

Tonight Is So Right For Love ★ ★ ★
With its unusual waltz-like signature, the melody to this tune was adapted by Joe Lilly from Tales from the Vienna Woods by Johann Strauss. This shouldn't work, given the strange notion of an Austrian-styled rock'n'roll waltz, but, thanks to Elvis doing his very best, it does.

What's She Really Like ★★
Lyrically a bit cheesy: one wonders how Elvis kept a straight face with lines like "Her lips are so thrillable / I can't describe her kiss in words of one syllable". In the end, this is inoffensive pop, but you get the feeling that Elvis really had his work cut out, on material that really doesn't pass muster.

Frankfort Special ★★
Despite the exhortations of having "A special way to go", this track (by Sid Wayne and Sherman Edwards) is fairly unremarkable. At least it paints a convincing aural picture of a train rolling down the track, which is enough to see it filed under the category of pleasant, but unmemorable.

GI Blues ★★★
Understandably 'GI Blues' draws heavily on the King's experiences with the US Army in Germany for inspiration. Not a bad track, it is perhaps most notable for the effective imitation of an army drill sergeant from those renowned backing vocalists, The Jordanaires.

Wooden Heart ★★★★
One of the better Elvis recordings from this period, 'Wooden Heart' also bears a European influence, this time from Germany. Based on an old German folk song – 'Muss Ich Denn Zum Stadele Naus' – it is carried along by a truly delightful melody and a charming performance from the recently demobbed GI.

Pocketful Of Rainbows ★★
A pleasant enough tune and a sweet little ditty, 'Pocketful Of Rainbows' could well border on the twee for most tastes – especially when set against the best blues/rock'n'roll in Presley's repertoire. No gold at the end of this rainbow.

Shoppin' Around ★★
With its upbeat rock'n'roll sound, 'Shoppin' Around' is, like the

title track, pretty light-hearted pop fare. No menace or danger to be found here, so consequently this song doesn't particularly excite.

Big Boots ★ ★

Depending on your outlook, this is either a charming, softly-sung lullaby, which is beautifully delivered from Elvis to a child. You may, on the other hand, find it straying a tad too close to novelty. It has the benefit of the doubt–just!

Didja' Ever ★ ★

1, 2, 3, 4... Let's all march military style. 'Didja' Ever' provides one-time fun, but despite Presley's best efforts, repeated listens betray it as a bit of a goofy novelty tune. Unfortunately, Elvis is caught out at first base on this one. More effective, it has to be said, with visuals in the cinema.

Blue Suede Shoes ★ ★ ★ ★

Even in this less than exalted company, 'Blue Suede Shoes' remains an unimpeachable rock'n'roll classic. Enough said.

Doin' The Best I Can ★ ★ ★ ★

A highlight, 'Doin the Best I Can' is a delicate doo-wop styled arrangement with lovely soft, lilting vocals from Elvis and some effective harmonica. It makes for an attractive confection – nothing hackneyed to be found here. Instead it's a little hidden gem.

Blue Hawaii
(1961)

Tracklisting: Blue Hawaii / Almost Always True / Aloha Oe / No More / Can't Help Falling In Love / Rock-a-Hula Baby / Moonlight Swim / Ku-u-i-po (Hawaiian Sweetheart) / Ito Eats / Slicin' Sand / Hawaiian Sunset / Beach Boy Blues / Island of Love / Hawaiian Wedding Song

Blue Hawaii ★ ★ ★
An Hawaiian-styled ballad confection tailored specifically for this soundtrack album, which is notable for some clever Hawaiian guitarr, juxtaposing the familiar Elvis croon against a loved one. Not particularly memorable when compared to the standout tracks that would follow....

Almost Always True ★ ★ ★
A medium paced rocker, although lyrically a bit too cute – see the "I resisted / Even though my arm was twisted" couplet. It has lashings of crazy saxophone and those omnipresent Hawaiian sounds layered on top. Entertaining, in a daft, seductive sing-along type way.

Aloha Oe ★ ★ ★ ★
This is a truly beautiful reading of a song written by the last reigning Queen of Hawaii. Sung partly in Hawaiian and partly in English, Elvis in this performance is simply happy to be one part of an all-male voice choir. A piece of traditional Hawaiian culture rendered Elvis-style that conjures up the majesty of the Hawaiian Islands.

No More ★ ★ ★
Vaguely reminiscent of the backing to 'It's Now or Never', with

its operatic, Neapolitan-styled pretensions, 'No More' is a sweet and sincere Elvis take of this Don Robertson-penned tune.

Can't Help Falling In Love ★ ★ ★ ★ ★

A trickling piano and some splendid Hawaiian guitar work accompany Elvis in his strong middle range register. The wonderful, heavenly feel of this song is supplied by the backing vocals from the excellent Jordanaires. With the lyrics full of romantic imagery, it's no wonder that this is one of Presley's best-loved ballads. Yet another standout track in the Elvis canon – coming to a wedding near you.

Rock-a-Hula Baby ★ ★ ★ ★

Instantly catchy, this Hawaiian-influenced rock number features Elvis' signature playful low-register 'Teddy Bear' vocal on a chorus that really hooks the listener in. To complete proceedings, it has a slow, tongue-in-cheek blues ending reminiscent of 'Jailhouse Rock'. Now everybody do the 'Boxcar Shuffle'.

Moonlight Swim ★ ★

Ladies, take a 'Moonlight Swim' with Elvis the Pelvis and he will 'keep you warm' on this gentle serenade with fluttery Hawaiian embellishments. 'Moonlight Swim', although marred by some slightly irksome female backing, is still an acceptable piece of Hawaiian hokum.

Ku-u-i-po (Hawaiian Sweetheart) ★ ★

Almost like a lullaby, but featuring, as it does, some saccharine sweet lyrics, the song is no more than the customary set-piece Elvis croon, this time to his 'Hawaiian Sweetheart'. Beautifully sung as always, and with a nice touch in Hawaiian pronunciation on the chorus.

Ito Eats ★ ★

There is a calypso feel to this infectious track, which together with some frenetic, pounding bongo drums, make for a pleasant

sounding sing-along that, at just under two minutes, doesn't outstay its welcome.

Slicin' Sand ★ ★ ★
'Slicin' Sand' is a song that recalls Elvis' rock'n'roll heyday, as the feel of 'Blue Suede Shoes' is echoed in the snappy stop-start lyrics, the wild electric guitar solo and the trademark Elvis vocal theatrics of yore. A slight, but well-sung track.

Hawaiian Sunset ★ ★ ★
There's not much on 'Hawaiian Sunset' to distinguish it from the other similar-flavoured ballads to be found elsewhere on this album. The stunning vocal harmonies alone, however, make this track worth the price of entry.

Beach Boy Blues ★ ★ ★
On the lighter end of the blues spectrum, this song contains an almost sing-along midsection and it has clever lyrics from Tepper and Bennett. There is some good harmonica and another decent bluesy vocalisation – one of the King's specialties.

Island of Love ★ ★ ★
Aloha to Hawaii: again we find this ballad mining the same vein that Presley had already established on tracks like 'Hawaiian Sunset' et al. The gentle sway of the palm trees makes this song appealing, but not intoxicating.

Hawaiian Wedding Song ★ ★ ★ ★ ★
Elvis takes the plaudits, without doubt, for the definitive version of the 'Hawaiian Wedding Song'. His treatment embraces traditional Hawaiian instrumentation and, for each line the King sings in English, the backing vocalists repeat them in Hawaiian. The song takes full advantage of Elvis' vocal range, in particular on the higher and cascading notes, and yet there is no hint of any strain in his voice. Hawaii 5-0.

Girls! Girls! Girls!
(1963)

Tracklisting: Girls! Girls! Girls! / I Don't Want To Be Tied / Where Do You Come From / I Don't Want To / We'll Be Together / Earth Boy / Return to Sender / Because Of Love / Thanks To The Rolling Sea / Song Of The Shrimp / The Walls Have Ears / We're Comin' In Loaded

Girls! Girls! Girls! ★ ★
This track certainly has the right credentials, as it was written by venerated songwriters Lieber & Stoller and features a splendid sax solo from Boots Randolph, together with some warm and resonate backing vocals on the chorus. It's unfortunate, then, that the song never quite matches up to the sum of its parts.

Where Do You Come From ★ ★ ★
Featuring a familiar mournful piano motif, 'Where Do You Come From' is another above average ballad, with a quivering vocal line from Presley. In this number, the Colonel's protégé demonstrates how his voice had developed since the days of 'Hound Dog'. An oft-neglected gem.

I Don't Want To ★ ★ ★
A classy ballad, in true Elvis fashion, but one that this time pitches the American Icon into an altogether more soulful country and is all the better for it. Even better when compared to the inconsequential fluff that was 'Song of the Shrimp'.

We'll Be Together ★ ★
A bit of a late-night serenade, 'We'll Be Together' has a definite Italian twist with lyrics full of romantic sentiment. The sound of a mellower Elvis, this syrupy love song was not one designed to make the parents recoil in horror. Pleasant enough.

Earth Boy ★

It's hard to defend this one – it's a lurch into novelty territory that deserves to be quickly glossed over. "Earth boy needs angel" sings Elvis, but it will take a lot more than that to save this song. The devil – not even in disguise!

Return To Sender ★ ★ ★ ★ ★

The sound of Elvis on back top form, 'Return To Sender' is a simply sublime moment in pop. Take an assured, joyous vocal, combine it with a universal lyric on a love lost, add a catchy sing-along chorus with bouncy interjections of sax – and eureka, you have a stone in the wall classic that continues to endure.

Because Of Love ★ ★

Again, this is pleasant enough – although ultimately superficial – early-60s Elvis pop, which in the final analysis does not satisfy. The sort of autopilot stuff that would quickly be rendered past its sell-by date before the mid-part of the decade.

Song Of The Shrimp ★

These truly dire lyrics could, in the best light, be taken as a joke. You want evidence? Take the line "Goodbye Mama Shrimp" as evidence for the prosecution come Judgment Day on this hackneyed song. Case closed. What was the great man thinking?

The Walls Have Ears ★ ★

Although in truth, this is not one of Presley's better entries – opening as it does with a cheesy marching beat – 'The Walls Have Ears' does possess a lively flamenco-style backing, which makes it distinctive –but alas, not definitive.

We're Comin' In Loaded ★ ★

A useful, if hackneyed, close to the album.

It Happened At The World's Fair
(1963)

Tracklisting: It Happened At The World's Fair / Beyond The Bend / Relax / Take Me To The Fair / They Remind Me Too Much Of You / One Broken Heart For Sale / I'm Falling In Love Tonight / Cotton Candy Land / World Of Our Own / How Would You Like To Be / Happy Ending

It Happened At The World's Fair ★ ★

A predictably upbeat opener, 'It Happened…' doesn't really stand up to repeated listens.

Beyond The Bend ★ ★ ★

A slight song when compared to the heavyweights in the Elvis songbook: nevertheless, this still provides some enjoyment, as it goes along with a nice groove and tempo. The interplay between the Elvis vocal and the musicians providing the backing is pleasing.

Relax ★ ★ ★

Elvis excels himself on 'Relax', and he obviously had a ball during the recording, as this seductive and sexy pseudo-blues number is a fun listen. There is some nice jazz guitar work from Tiny Timbrell, along with the dual pianos of Dudley Brooks and Don Robertson on a sonic palette that serves up one of Elvis's finer 60s moments.

Take Me To The Fair ★ ★

More lightweight material, indicative of the general slump in the King's output. The sound of the auto-pilot kicking in – there would be others in the pop firmament on both sides of the Atlantic who would realise and take advantage… disappointing.

They Remind Me Too Much Of You ★ ★ ★ ★

In Elvis' later works, the maxim has always been that his better recordings were the ballads. That rings true here, as 'They Remind Me Too Much Of You' has the feel of discovering buried treasure. Composed by Don Robertson (who also contributes some nifty organ), this track is furnished by truly astonishing vocal fireworks from Presley and inhabits an orbit not too far removed from the 'Chapel in the Moonlight'. The man sure loved to sing!

One Broken Heart For Sale ★ ★ ★

'One Broken Heart For Sale' shares the same antecedents as Elvis's previous hit record 'Return to Sender' – only this time revisited as a bit of a Jackie Wilson pastiche. 'One Broken Heart For Sale' is a catchy and upbeat tune, which certainly brings out a decent performance from Presley with his voice in fine fettle, coming across loud and clear. Don Robertson is the notable contributor on the piano parts.

I'm Falling In Love Tonight ★ ★ ★

"When love let me down before / I said I was through / But I'm falling in love tonight / With you", sung in the solid ballad-style by East Tupelo's most famous resident. 'I'm Falling in Love Tonight' was contributed (again) by Don Robertson and in the Elvis ballad stakes, it's none too shabby.

Cotton Candy Land ★ ★ ★

OK, so much of Elvis's later fare could be varied in quality and 'Cotton Candy Land' is another prime example of this principle. It's light-hearted and, of all things, a song aimed at the children: guaranteed, therefore, to leave most rock'n'roll purists wringing their hands in disbelief! If, however, you can get past those prejudices, you'll get the benefit of Elvis's dramatic treatment and great singing.

World Of Our Own ★ ★

Not a heavyweight song, but certainly not offensive…

How Would You Like To Be ★

The antithesis to Elvis' earlier rockers, on songs like this, one wonders at the singer's control and professionalism, as 'How Would You Like To Be' is below-par and second-rate material. Not worthy of the King's attention or yours.

Happy Ending ★ ★ ★

It has to be said that Elvis's singing on 'Happy Ending' – otherwise a bit of an also-ran in the Presley pantheon – is positively spectacular. As the arrangement shifts up a gear, he gets even more impassioned. Never has a title been so prophetic to these ears.

Fun In Acapulco
(1963)

Tracklisting: Fun In Acapulco / Vino Dinero Y Amor / Mexico / El Toro / Marguerita / Bullfighter Was A Lady / No Room To Rhumba In A Sports Car / I Think I'm Gonna Like It Here / Bossa Nova Baby / You Can't Say No In Acapulco / Guadalajara / Love Me Tonight / Slowly But Surely

Fun In Acapulco ★ ★ ★ ★

Showing, as with his Hawaiian sojourn, that Elvis could be comfortable in another musical country, 'Fun In Acapulco' does not disappoint. Slightly odd fade-out notwithstanding, this track is among one of the King's finest presentations, with some lovely percussive elements and Tiny Timbrell's mandolin to savour.

Vino Dinero Y Amor ★ ★ ★

Tequila drenched, with exclamations from the Amigos (sounding rather like 'Viva, viva' – an early precursor to 'Viva Las Vegas', perhaps?), this song chugs along at a fast pace. It has alcoholic bonhomie in abundance, and coupled with rattlesnake percussion, you can't help but be swept along. It's not bad at all.

Bullfighter Was A Lady ★ ★

With its brassy opening, Elvis tells the tale of Pedro the killer bull, who goes soft when he becomes smitten with the female bullfighter of the title. Despite the frequent cries of 'Olé!' from the Mexican Amigos on the backing vocals, 'Bullfighter Was a Lady' is nothing more than a Latin-styled curio. Fairly preposterous.

Mexico ★ ★

All very well, this Latin malarkey, but 'Mexico' is swathed in rather annoying Tijuana brass and a nagging woodblock percussion on the intro. Needless to say, this being Presley's whistlestop Mexican tour, the song goes all out for the obvious lyrical reference points. Sorry to report – this is about as satisfying as last night's warmed-up chili.

El Toro ★

Elvis tells the tale of bullfighting matadors in 'El Toro', which for all its dramatic touches and attempts at authenticity, is still found wanting. Not a song that you would want to repeat and definitely not a forerunner for inclusion in the numerous Elvis best-of collections. One for the truly committed only.

Marguerita ★ ★ ★

A Don Robertson (boy – that man was a prolific songsmith) song, this comes with added Latino feeling – thanks to the combination of prominent Spanish guitars and Mexican brass in the mix. The gentle percussion in the build up to Elvis's dramatic and passionate cry of "Marguerita" is also worthwhile.

(There's) No Room To Rhumba In A Sports Car ★ ★ ★
'(There's) No Room To Rhumba in a Sports Car' is lovably daft. Elvis is in a playful mood on what is intended to be nothing more than a light-hearted piece of nonsense. If you're after deep symbolism, then don't hitch a ride in this car.

I Think I'm Gonna Like It Here ★ ★ ★
More fun to be had here as Elvis presents a lolloping number thanks to some bongos, tambourine and rattling piano. Again, the Amigos provide 'hush, hush' on the vocal backing to Elvis's chorus, which takes you into his confidence when he stops to declare the song's title. He's right – there are worse places to stay.

Bossa Nova Baby ★ ★ ★ ★
A swinging twister, 'Bossa Nova Baby' (from the pen of Lieber & Stoller and originally a hit for the Clovers) is a work of genius, which brings together rock'n'roll with a frenetic and infectious bossa nova beat. A wonderfully inspired treatment and hugely danceable, the groovy keyboard work – which is worth the price of admission alone – as a counterpoint to the chorus, borders on the downright funky.

You Can't Say No In Acapulco ★ ★ ★
A sinuous Elvis smoulders like an international playboy on his way through 'You Can't Say No In Acapulco' – a smoky piece of sexy sassiness displaying oodles of roguish charm. You should only find yourself saying yes to the Latino Elvis.

Guadalajara ★ ★ ★
Elvis's version of 'Guadalajara' (a popular Mexican song) is a curio delivered by Presley in crystal-clear and fluent Spanish. 'Guadalajara' boasts a superb vocal accompaniment by the

Amigos, and it provides a declaration of Elvis's immense vocal versatility.

Love Me Tonight ★ ★
Another useful but forgettable mid-beat ballad.

Slowly But Surely ★ ★
Not a standout track, by any means.

Kissin' Cousins
(1964)

Tracklisting: Kissin' Cousins (No. 2) / Smokey Mountain Boy / There's Gold In The Mountains / One Boy Two Little Girls / Catchin' On Fast / Tender Feeling / Anyone (Could Fall In Love With You) / Barefoot Ballad / Once Is Enough / Kissin' Cousins (No. 1) / Echoes Of Love / Long Lonely Highway

Kissin' Cousins (No. 2) ★ ★ ★
Not a bad way to begin, 'Kissin' Cousins (No 2)' is a rock-plus-blues piece that has some nice drum patterns and electric guitar signatures (not too dissimilar to 'Route 66' in places). Elvis handles the somewhat goofy subject matter, "Well, we're kissin' cousins and that's what make it alright" with an assured delivery and even duets with himself on the chorus. A catchy, let's-all-sing-along-with-Elvis-type number.

Smokey Mountain Boy ★ ★
Shame – not even Elvis can coax any magic out of this lame marching song by Millrose & Rosenblatt (Lieber & Stoller they're not!). Confine this boy to the farthest reaches of the King's back catalogue and quickly close the door.

There's Gold In The Mountains ★ ★

Yet another attempt at a catchy singalong. 'There's Gold In The Mountains' doesn't scale any heights, being fairly mediocre, and as for finding gold – you'd be better off taking your shovel digging elsewhere.

One Boy Two Little Girls ★ ★ ★

You would struggle to place, 'One Boy, Two Little Girls' at the top of the Elvis ballad pile. That said, the man with the quiff does manage to convince you that this slow number is actually better than it is. Presley deserves some credit for that, as he once again transforms some unexceptional material into something bordering on decent.

Catchin' On Fast ★ ★

'Catchin' On Fast' tries and fails to recapture the former glories of Elvis's rock'n'roll past. It's Presley by numbers and never gets beyond its uninspired tableau of rock clichés.

Tender Feeling ★ ★ ★ ★

By this time, you can't really blame Elvis for sounding a bit below par. On 'Tender Feeling', however, he manages to perk up sufficiently, as the song is a tune based on a traditional civil war ballad ('Shenandoah') and has the added bonus of a really good hook on the melody line. Love this song tenderly – it's the highlight.

Anyone (Could Fall In Love With You) ★ ★

A slushy song on a slushy album…

Barefoot Ballad ★

On this appalling piece of hokum, we get the thrill (or otherwise) of Elvis Presley counting his dead toes. Surely that would be enough to consign 'Barefoot Ballad' to the dumpster? Alas no, as all this takes place to the joyous accompaniment of a nose flute! A career nadir.

Once Is Enough ★ ★ ★

Another glance back into the past and Elvis's heyday. A moderately entertaining song that certainly improves on the other offerings on this album – it has a certain charm to recommend it.

Kissin' Cousins (No. 1) ★ ★

This song has the catchy sing-along melody to please, but the lyrics are goofy hokum. I'm not sure a retread of this song was necessary.

Echoes Of Love ★ ★

A maudlin Elvis sings, "Though you are gone / I still wear your ring / They're playing the song we used to sing / Echoes of love / Echoes of love / Are coming to me out of the past". The end result? Below-par sentimentality that doesn't live long in the memory.

Long Lonely Highway ★ ★

It's a long road, all right, especially with songs like this one on the 8-track player…

Roustabout

(1964)

Tracklisting: Roustabout / Little Egypt / Poison Ivy League / Hard Knocks / It's A Wonderful World / Big Love Big Heartache / One Track Heart / It's Carnival Time / Carny Town / There's A Brand New Day On The Horizon / Wheels On My Heels

Roustabout ★ ★ ★

A laid-back presentation of Elvis the roving motorbikin' roustabout. The title track is not exactly a hell's angel, but then

again, it's no moped either. This song (by the trio of Grant, Baum & Kaye) is quite an effective mid-60s supper dish swinger.

Little Egypt ★ ★ ★ ★

"Hey yeah" smirks Elvis during the story of belly dancer Little Egypt. His version of the Lieber & Stoller song (originally recorded by the Coasters) possesses great lines such as, "She had a ruby on her tummy and a diamond on her toes", which Elvis sings with a natural charm and wit. Excellent bass (reminiscent of a 60s spy movie) and copious amounts of saxophone (Boots Randolph again) make for an infectious mid-paced groove: all combine to present Presley in his best mid-60s light.

Poison Ivy League ★ ★

A bitter swipe at the 'Rah Rah Boys' of the Poison Ivy League, this song is too nice to be anything other than forgettable filler.

Hard Knocks ★ ★ ★

'Hard Knocks' (from the pen of Joe Byers) holds the attention and, with a subject matter about growing up in poverty, it enables Elvis to embody his vocal delivery with bags of attitude (perhaps from recollections of his own childhood). Ably supported by the outstanding harmonies of the Jordanaires, Presley is further complemented by excellent guitar and drum work.

It's A Wonderful World ★ ★

Not the Louis Armstrong song. Instead, this is a bustling carnival scene-setter cut from the same cloth as 'It's Carnival Time'.

Big Love Big Heartache ★ ★ ★

That this big ballad works at all is largely thanks to the vocal perspiration of Presley and the backing vocals from the Jordanaires. Once again, Elvis's vocal talents place him above less supreme beings and it saves this song from being an also-ran.

One Track Heart ★ ★
Cue more Herculean vocal efforts from Elvis and the Jordanaires, 'One Track Heart' is propelled along by some imaginative drums and a performance from the King that conceives to sprinkle some of his fairy dust on a fairly ordinary number.

It's Carnival Time ★ ★
Evocative of spit and sawdust, this track breezes along on some cheesy organ work. Elvis acts as the master of ceremonies on this inconsequential piece of cinematic filler.

Carny Town ★ ★
Based as it is on the 'Entry of the Gladiators' – a theme made instantly familiar by circus troupes around the world – 'Carny Town' is indicative of the kind of musical straitjacket that enveloped Elvis, stifling his undoubted artistry, in the mid-60s.

There's A Brand New Day On The Horizon ★ ★ ★
Another Joe Byers composition, this song is a life-affirming gospel song, in which Presley declares that he wants to tell, "Old Heartaches to pack his bags and go". Increasing in tempo with each verse, this has an infectious groove that's bound to dispel those black clouds.

Wheels On My Heels ★ ★ ★
Sharing similar DNA to its predecessor, Presley has to keep everything moving in a reference to his motorbike and life on the open road. With a quintessential Elvis vocal inflection on the line "rolling along", the proceedings bounce along at a fair old lick, buoyed by strong saxophone work.

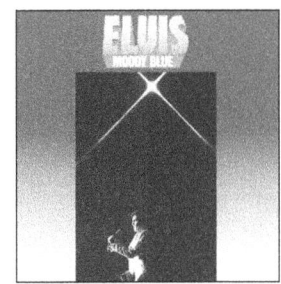

Moody Blue
(1977)

Tracklisting: Unchained Melody / If You Love Me (Let Me Know) / Little Darlin' / He'll Have To Go / Let Me Be There / Way Down / Pledging My Love / Moody Blue / She Thinks I Still Care / It's Easy For You

Unchained Melody ★ ★ ★

'Unchained Melody' – probably the most ubiquitous song in pop history – has been covered many times, but few can touch the peerless version by The Righteous Brothers. Although the King doesn't quite match those heights, his reading of this pop standard is passionate enough to register. Elvis is on impressive form, particularly his singing on the lines, "I hunger for your touch / Are you still mine?" Still an amazing vocal talent, and there is enough here to send a shiver down the spine.

If You Love Me (Let Me Know) ★ ★ ★

Elvis had always been an intuitive interpreter of songs by other artists, and never better than on this upbeat track. Previously a country hit for Olivia Newton John, of all people, 'If You Love Me' is a pure pop gem that showcases a fine backup band on top form.

Little Darlin' ★ ★ ★

A happy-go-lucky dance song. 'Little Darlin'' is a cover of a 50s tune that Elvis, for one, doesn't take too seriously and the proceedings are all the better for it. His tongue-in-cheek delivery certainly gives the song a light-hearted feeling that entertains.

He'll Have To Go ★ ★ ★

Following the reverie of the previous song, 'He'll Have To Go' starts with "Put your sweet lips a little closer to the phone /

Just pretend we are together all alone". A sad song that features the deep, bluesy tone of the Elvis voice and pulls at the heart strings.

Let Me Be There ★ ★ ★ ★
An upbeat tune and a terrific Elvis performance in front of a live audience. The girls scream all the way through it and demand an encore. The audience are obviously enjoying themselves and so will you. The voice is, once again, immaculate. Close enough to be the standout track.

Way Down ★ ★ ★ ★ ★
'Way Down' is truly vintage 70s Elvis and, as his last big hit, a mighty way to bow out. A truly dynamic song, all at once funky, bluesy and exuberant, it demonstrates the full range of Elvis's singing talent. Even the cheesy, low register backing vocals – repeating the title of the song – work somehow. A masterpiece.

Pledging My Love ★ ★ ★
A slow ballad, 'Pledging My Love' is an update of the song by blues artist Johnny Ace. Filled with compassion, Elvis really puts his heart and soul into this one. Lines like "Making you happy is my desire" showcase Elvis in a fine romantic mood.

Moody Blue ★ ★ ★ ★
One thing is for sure, the King is really into this catchy song, with an appealing intro, about a complicated lady that he just can't figure out. It's a narrative song that's well written and when, at one stage, he asks "Tell me if I am getting through", the answer is yes.

She Thinks I Still Care ★ ★ ★ ★
More than any other song, this song evokes the King's personal situation, particularly when Elvis asks, "Just because I asked a friend about her / Just because I spoke her name somewhere /

Just because I rang her number my mistake today / You know she thinks I still care". George Jones, eat your heart out.

It's Easy For You ★ ★ ★
'It's Easy For You' sings Elvis in this slow lament for the loss of a woman he loved. "I had a wife and I had children / I threw them all away" is sung with a poignancy that descends into pathos, as the King opens up his heart and pours out his troubles. Not exactly easy listening.

DJ FONTANA IN HIS OWN WORDS

INTERVIEW CONDUCTED BY GARY MOORE

I met Scotty, Bill and Elvis at the Louisiana hayride down in Shreveport, Louisiana. I had heard their records, they were playing rock in that one area and one of the managers called me there one day and said "I want you to listen to this record". So I went to his office and they played it and I said "How many guys they got playing in this band?" and they said "Just 3 guys" and it sounded like 5 or 6 people with the echo and everything and I said "Boy that's awfully good." So anyway, they come in and Scotty said "would you like to work with those tonight?" and I said "Yeah, well that's why I'm here".

I said "Let's go back into the dressing room and kind of talk about it". So Elvis got his guitar and Scotty and Bill and they just played a little bit and I said "Yeah, we can do that then". So we did it that night and he'd come back in a few weeks later and we did it again. Two or three weeks and he'd come back in and out. So that's how it basically got started. Just by accident I happened to be there.

Q What were your first impressions of Elvis as a musician? What did you make of him?
Well, his voice was so unusual for that time period and his clothes were unusual – his dress with the peg pants and all that stuff and stripes down his pants leg. And he was a good looking kid, a good looking guy and I said "Hey this guy might do ok – who knows?" he had that certain charisma about him that there was no way for him to miss, no way.

Q **What was the music scene like then? Was Elvis ahead of his time?**

Yeah, well I think he was a little bit ahead of his time. We were all still listening to the big bands – Woody Herman, Stan Kenton, those kinds of guys. The Dorsey Brothers – that's all we had basically on radio. They had a couple of blues stations but they didn't get out very far – 5,000 miles and stuff like that and so we were really into the big band listening.

Q **What kind of drummer are you yourself? Where did you get a lot of your influences?**

From the big bands, listening to those guys play and watching them, if they'd come in town. Sometimes every now and again there would be a big orchestra come through town on a one nighter. And we'd all go out and see them play and you learn a little bit from each one of the guys.

Q **How did it feel going from behind the curtain to in front of the curtain?**

Oh it was different yeah it was just a farce I think. Basically the country acts and the country programmes wasn't really for me

with drums at all. So they weren't sure how the people would take us so they'd say "Well you stand back there and play" and I'd say "Well that's alright with me" you get paid the same money you know. And every couple of weeks they'd say "Well, just bring a snare drum out and bring a cymbal out" and by the time we'd got through with Elvis they had the whole set out he said "Just bring them all out". That's what he wanted and that's what Elvis wanted so I guess maybe they kind of figured they'd better go along with his wishes I guess cos he was drawing a lot of people in there by then.

Q So obviously what you were used to was different from what Elvis was playing. What kind of music was being played, where was the influence coming from?
I think they'd come from a lot of black groups being from a Memphis area and he'd listened to a lot of black radio programmes. Scotty was a kind of a blues, jazz player he wanted to be and Bill was just an all-round bass player, that's not country not pop just, the feel of that's what he did, he had good feeling to his bass playing.

Q What kind of drums were you using? What kind of sound were you trying to achieve?
Well I had Gretsch drums and so that's all I really knew, what they sounded like and I used them on all the early records – we did a lot here in RCAB here, did a lot in California - I'd ship them on a plane. And back then you could do that without them getting hurt, they really took care of them where nowadays they throw them around so bad I wouldn't dare send anything in that luggage like that. But they really took care of equipment, all the equipment.

Q Was there anything different about the way you played drums on the music like time signatures or was it just straight hit?

No straight hit basically - you just play what you want to play basically. All the stuff we did early was hit arrangements. He'd play an acetate right here in the middle of the floor and he'd say "Yeah well we'll keep that one" and they he'd throw another one on a pile over there, he didn't like that. And he'd say "Well let's see what we can do with this one" and we'd pick out something and he'd say "Just play it and if it doesn't feel right we'll get another feel". It was up to him basically. Usually he was right so I'd say "Well you want me to play this?" "No don't play this play something else". So you just kind of listened to what he wanted, that's what we did.

Q Tell me a bit about Heartbreak Hotel and Jailhouse Rock, Teddy Bear…
Heartbreak was done not too far from here actually and it was a kind of an old ex-church, cathedral like – it was a small place but that was what they used it as at one time. And there wasn't a so-called echo chambers like they have even in this studio and they ran some mike cords and mikes down the hallway for echo on the record, that's how the sound of that, they wanted to get the old Sun sound on the Heartbreak Hotel but it just wasn't the same. It never was the same. But they tried.

Q Did you do any recordings in here? Can you tell us more about where we are right now?
We're in RCAB – we probably did hundreds of them right here in this studio – Stuck on You, some I can't remember all of them now – you got a list? There was just hundreds of them.

Q And what did you make of Elvis as a person and a musician and an actor?
I thought he was good – he was a good musician, he knew in his mind what he wanted to hear and sometimes he'd have a hard time explaining it to you because he wasn't the best musician – none of us were good musicians but we knew kind of what his

thinking was so we basically went along with him and somehow or other it worked, it really worked well.

Q Do you think this Elvis phenomenon happened overnight or did it evolve gradually?
No it took a little while. But we worked some real some dives you might say and we worked some high school gyms, some little Friday night football stadiums so we did a lot of that for I guess a year and a half or so. It didn't really bust right open until we went up to do the Dorsey Shows. And then people saw him and he kept getting bigger and bigger and bigger and then we did the Sinatra show and we did this show and that show, all the main television programmes of that time period, we did them all.

Q What was life on the road like when you were travelling around?
Well, we had one car, me, Scotty and Bill and Elvis had all our instruments in that one car. Sometimes he'd bring Jean Smith with him who was his cousin, sometimes Billy, another cousin and other times Red West so it was a car full of people and instruments but somehow or other we all got in there and we had a great time. Well you couldn't do much just sit there and talk. You couldn't move around much cos it was just too crowded, too many people.

Q Tell us about your fellow musicians, Scotty and Bill tell us a bit about what they're like as musicians to work with.
They're easy to work with, all of the guys were easy to work with. They knew what he wanted cos they knew him a little while before I did so we all just kind of played it basically by ear. Scotty had to play rhythm and lead at the same time and that made it hard for him. So when I joined the band he said "I'm glad you got here cos, boy, I always have to do it all". You know which, that's what he did. He said "Now I can count, you know

play more lead or whatever without losing the whole bottom end of it" and Bill's slapping his bass. We had a great sound I thought.

Q And Scotty as a manager?
He was a road manager for a while and the reason for that I think is that you could go up and say "Elvis we want to do this benefit". "OK I'll do it". He'd do 10 benefits, he'd say "Yeah yeah, just call us, call us". And they finally got him to say "We can't do them all" so I think it was Sam or one of the guys told him "Somebody's gonna have to be manager, somebody's gonna have to be a bad guy". He said "We can't do it", and Scotty said "Well, I'll do it". So then I'd have to ask Scotty and we did a few things but you can't do them all. You know we tried to do the best we could but we just couldn't get around to doing all the free ones.

Q Were you making money with Elvis back then?
No we never made any money, that wasn't the point. We were just trying to do something that we thought was gonna be a hit, cut good records – we didn't make a lot of money at all, it could have been a lot better but we had management problems and one thing and another so you can't argue with the world so we'd just say "That's ok" and we were having a good time, we were young and doing pictures and TV shows, how many guys get the chance to do that.

Q Shows, that's with Scotty, Bill and yourself?
Yeah, yeah

Q There's loads of songs – do any of these songs stand out? Tell me about the studio recordings, did it take loads of times to do?
No not really once he got started sometimes they'd call a session here at the RCAB at 6 o'clock in the evening and he might not show up until 11 o'clock and then he'd sing, we'd all do round

the piano, sing gospel for a couple more hours and all the higher ups were getting panicky spending a lot of money and that made them a little nervous. But once he got started he'd say "Ok guys time to go to work", and he was ready. We'd listen to the acetate and everybody would take little notes of what you wanted to play in our own minds and he'd say "Well let's try it" and we'd kick it off and if he didn't like it he'd say "Well now let's do something else". It's a matter of hit and miss just whatever he thought what he wanted to hear that's what he got.

Q Was there room for experimentation?
Yeah, nobody pushed us cos he wouldn't have allowed that in the first place. He'd say if everybody's uncomfortable and everybody's uptight we're not going to cut good records. If he felt the room was uptight "Knock it off guys – we'll get a bite to eat and take off for an hour or so then come back"

Q I read that you guys were being paid hourly so he'd make a joke with you just so you could make a few bucks.
Yeah well when we were doing the soundtracks for the pictures and he'd come around every now and again and say "Are you guys making any money yet" and we'd say "No Elvis cos it's going too fast". You'd get paid by the hour in 3 hour segments and we'd say "No it's moving kinda fast" and he'd say "OK I'll take care of that" and he'd go to play the piano, go to sing gospel a couple of hours – they were still, the clock was still clicking you see and after a few hours I'd say "What do you think now?" and he'd say "OK we can get started again", you know. And every so often he'd stop us "We'll take a break" but the clock was still ticking – he was good at that.

Q Tell us about your roles in the movies and what you thought of his acting.
Well, our roles weren't much – none of us were actors. Bill wanted to be an actor, he really did. Bill could have been a good

character actor he really could. None of us had any big lines or anything – Bill had a few, me and Scotty never did talk much on the scene itself, we just happened to be in a lot of scenes. Bill had a couple of little acts that he did on Loving You. He did a good job, he could have been a good actor he sure could.

Q How do you rate Scotty as a guitarist?
He was probably one of the finest guitar players you ever wanted to run into. The way he played was so unique from all the other guys, it was different. He played the thumb and the rhythm and just – if you could hear his records you could tell it's Scotty, there's no question about it. All the guitar players haven't figured out what he's doing yet.

Q He's very modest when he comes to talking about himself.
Yeah, well he played some really good things on them records. And all the big guitar players, they talk about him all the time. How many good licks he played and his originality of what he was doing, they talk about him all the time.

Q Do you think that Shake, Rattle and Roll was the world's first glimpse of Elvis on television?
Well, we had done a couple more songs before that I believe on one of those shows but I don't remember which one was which now.

Q Why do you think his performances on television made such an impact?
Well he was different, absolutely different and his clothes were different. Like I said earlier, he was a good looking guy and that got all the ladies on his side of course and also he could sing and that was the main thing and the little band we had, the trio, was a good little trio. We played things that he needed so we stuck very close to his method of singing. He had a unique voice and all you had to do was just lay back and not do a lot and let him sing.

Q Was his dancing and his lip snarl always there or did he have to develop that?

No, you know that dancing, when he first started he didn't dance around too much but a couple of times he was moving around a little bit and we got through and he said "Why are all those kids screaming and hollering" and we said "Well you're dancing, you're moving around" and he said "Oh am I?". I don't think he realised it. So after that he did more of it - he could see the reaction in the kids by then and he said "Oh that's pretty good I'll just do some more".

Q Is it right that the song Hound Dog took 70 takes to complete?

No no no no, I don't know where they get that from but then they said 35, but actually what they were calling takes was a count of 1, 2, 3, 4 "No wrong tempo", or you play 2 or 3 bars then something would happen "No". They counted all those little stops and starts as a take. And I think he finally went back I'm not sure of the cut but it was way down on the 5th or 6th cut he took. But it wasn't nothing like 35 or 70 – I don't know where they got that from. They just counted all that stuff on tape.

Q Can you or would you dispel any myths that are out there – is there any big myths that you can dispel, again like the one I've just said?

No not really – it's according to whose books you read of course. And I don't read them so I don't know who's writing what. I really don't pay that much attention to them. He treated me decent and he treated all of us decent so that's what we go by.

Q How long did you play with Elvis and when did it end?

I was with him 14 years actually. Scotty and Bill they started it completely, those 3 guys were the band. I joined them a little bit later and a little bit later The Jordanaires joined us down in Atlanta, Georgia and they stayed with us a long time so it was just a matter of getting people that you could get along with actually.

Q And tell us a bit about The Jordanaires – what did they bring to the music?
Well they helped us out a lot cos they were doing all the background parts, singing all the do-waps and to me it sounded like the horn section sometimes. They made it sound like we had a big band back there. Gordon played a little piano on some of the stage things and Hoyt Hawkins, he's passed away now, Hoyt played a little piano so it helped fill up the band.

Q Do you think the early television performances were good in formal musical terms?
Yeah I think they were, I don't know how, what else we could have done. Course like I said they still had their big bands behind us and everything. But still we were doing like we were supposed to do and that's what they were buying.

Q Do you think there was anything out of the ordinary in Elvis's version of Blue Suede Shoes and Tutti Frutti?
No. I listened to both Carl Perkins' and Elvis' and Carl had a superb version of it he really did, I think his was a little bit slower than ours but Elvis did a great job on it and Tutti Frutti he did a good job and I think he heard that from Little Richard – one of those guys had it out before we put it out. So, he was always listening to different artists and if he found a song he liked, he'd try it. And usually he was pretty good.

Q Heartbreak Hotel, do you think that was the first real Elvis classic?
Yeah I think so – that was the record - that got him, that got him off of Sun actually. We were on Sun he wasn't and with the Heartbreak that was like, even before it was released I think it was like a million – that was the first million selling record

for him which was pretty darn good. A new kid on the pike and there he is he's got a million seller.

Q What did When the Blue Moon Turns to Gold tell us about Elvis' gospel influence?

He was great on the gospel song, I've always said that, and he loved gospel music. Every chance he got to hear a gospel group and he would go. Years they used to have several gospel troops come through town all the time. And they played Memphis of course and he'd go back and see them, every one of them he knew all by heart, he knew them all by name and he just loved gospel music and that's where he got a lot of his feeling from.

Q Did Love Me Tender provide the first real indicator of Elvis' talent as an interpreter of ballads?

Yeah, that was a good record, that Love Me Tender. For his first movie I thought it was pretty darn decent.

Q Why do you think Elvis was such a phenomenon in the early days?

Well, he could sing, he was unusual – when he walked in a room you knew it was him. Like I said earlier he was a good looking guy so that might have been just a combination of all of it put together was probably what made it go so well.

Q Did Elvis' duet with Frank Sinatra demonstrate that the two were equals as performers?

I think they did a good job together. I think Sinatra kind of got on his side after a while, he wasn't sure about how they would like each other in other words. But they got on a show and they were laughing and grinning and having a good time in rehearsals and they all seemed like they really got along fine.

Q Why was the '68 comeback special or was the comeback special Elvis at his very best do you think?

I think so – I think the whole show was good. The segment

in the round was really good with the black little suit and all that stuff. No instruments, just Scotty's guitar and a couple of rhythm things. He looked good – that was the best I'd seen him look in a long time.

Q With songs like My Way, was there a danger Elvis had become too showbiz? Was his version as good as Sinatra's?
I think it was. Sinatra had a great version and Elvis had a great version so I think it was a toss up between the two, it's according to who you liked the best. And some of the fans liked Sinatra and some liked Elvis. So it was a mixture of all of it and I thought that both cuts were good.

Q What do you think were the musical highlights of Elvis' output in the 70's?
I wasn't around back then. You see I was gone in '68 so I can't answer those questions whatsoever. I thought that since he had to go to Vegas, he needed a show band, I mean he needed a production and that's what they were looking for and that's why he went over so well in Vegas.

Q American Trilogy – the ultimate Elvis song do you think?
I think so, I like that song myself. Micky Newberry did a great job on it and Elvis sung the fire out of it. A lot of people out there in the audience, you'd see them on that split screen and you could see these people out there crying cos he was very sincere about it.

Q Do the early 70s films of Elvis in concert do him justice as a performer?
Oh yeah, that's when he really got into the karate moves and the kicks and the big bands behind him and he really sounded good with that big band, he really did.

Q Do you think Elvis was a perfectionist in terms of his performance?

Oh yeah, he wanted everything exactly right. Even on his records he wanted it right. He'd say "No we have to do it again". You gotta remember way back then we only had mono tracks so there weren't no fixing nothing, you'd go back in and do the whole song again so we just kept going.

Q Aloha from Hawaii – the best example of a mature Elvis in concert?

That was another great concert but you know it's hard to say which one was the best cos there were all good. They made darn sure that he did a good job, course he made sure that he did a good job and the sound was good and the film was good and they all did great job – I can't say a darn thing bad about it.

Q Do you think the 70s Vegas repertoire was sufficiently challenging?

No, no, he was doing basically his old songs except different tempos and I think he threw away a lot of the vocals on those up tempo when it got so fast that nobody could understand what he was talking about half of the time. I think he should have done them originally where they were and do more of them if he had to but don't just rush through them. No I don't think that's a good idea.

Q Could the effect of Elvis' decline in health be seen in his later performances?

Well I didn't see him after a while anyhow. I knew that like everyone else you read the papers and you knew he was sick here and he was sick there. It seemed like every time he'd come to town he'd get sick and he ended up in the hospital and there was always something back and forth, it wasn't anything serious but it was just enough to figure he had been kind of not real well for the last few years.

Q I mean, were drugs a problem when you worked with him?

No, never saw them. In fact he didn't drink. Me, Scotty and Bill, we'd have a beer or two you know and that was about it.

Q Do you think Elvis was overrated or is he really the King in your opinion?

No he wasn't overrated by no means. He didn't like to be called the King but still he was the number 1 guy and he still is. I just got back from Denmark and Sweden and there's people over there that still love Elvis. Everywhere you go they love Elvis, after all these years he's passed away.

Q Do you remember where you were and how you felt when you heard he'd passed away?

I was at Sun Records actually, not Memphis but over at Belmont and Shelby Singleton had brought all this stuff out, all the Sun stuff and we were cutting somebody over there I don't remember who it was now and he came on the talkback about 4-4.30. He said "DJ" he said "We just heard Elvis had passed away" and he said "It's on the radio" he said "You want to call the session?" We were supposed to be through at 5 anyhow. I said "No, let's finish up". Costs a lot of money just to cancel a session you know, I said "No, no, we'll wait till 5 and then I'll run home". I didn't live too far from the studio at the time, maybe 10 minutes away. And I got on the phone and I tried to call everybody I knew, that was associated with Elvis at that time. Couldn't get any, everybody was out of pocket. Everybody was either in the air coming or going. So finally I got hold of Joe Esposito at the house finally and he said it's true. So I caught the next plane out the next morning, me and my wife and the kids we went down and spent the whole day with them you know, at the home and the next morning I had to leave actually I had to go to Virginia – I had some more sessions up there so Billy Smith took me out the back gate, and back to the airport, me and the family and I got back home that night about 10 or 11 o'clock, so it was a sad, sad day for everybody.

Q To sum up, is there anything you'd like to add about the whole time you were with Elvis and the whole time you were in the band?

Well the only thing is like I said, early on we all had a great time together. And I think the reason for that was we could all talk and sleep in the cars, stop and get a hamburger if you wanted to so that made it a little easier. As he got bigger and bigger and bigger, well we could feel that as we got bigger we couldn't get in the venues as easy. We had to have certain passes, certain security and all that stuff. And it made it hard for everybody and we only saw him actually on stage and he's off stage. But early on it was all driving and stopping for food and one thing and another, we had a lot of time to talk.

SCOTTY MOORE IN HIS OWN WORDS

INTERVIEW CONDUCTED BY GARY MOORE

Q Tell me about when you first picked up the guitar, when you were in the Navy – tell me about your influences.
Well I guess I started trying to play a little bit when I was around 9 or 10 years old, I got interested in it. I had three brothers, my three brothers and my dad all played string instruments and there was 14 years difference between me and the next one up the ladder. And so by the time I got to that age, everybody was gone, married or in the navy or whatever and I think one thing drove me was just being hard headed more than anything else.

Q And what kind of music were you interested in?
Any kind, it didn't matter. Course I heard a lot of country music back, coming off the farm and a lot of black music and I heard some popular music of course on the radio and stuff like that.

Q You have quite a unique style. How did you develop that unique style?
Just stealing from everybody I guess and putting it all together. If I've got a style - I never considered that I did. I tried to play the song, I tried to listen to the song cos I don't read music or at least as Chet Atkins used to say "You didn't read enough to hurt your playing." I tried to listen to a song and play something I'd think would fit the music or the way the guy was singing, you know, that way.

Q When did you first get involved with working with Elvis? When did you first meet him and what were your first impressions of him?
Well I had a group of my own in Memphis called The Starlite

Wranglers, which I had formed right after I had got out of the navy and we did one record at Sun and, when I found out there was a place there where you could make records, I went in and talked to Sam Phillips. He agreed to listen to the group and we went in and auditioned for him and at first, I always remember, the first thing he said was "Have you got any original material?" and we said "No." And he said "Well you got a good group, I like the group. If you get some original material, come back, I'd like to see what you got." And so me and my oldest brother and Doug Poindexter, we wrote 2 songs just over a few days and we went back and we did the record with Sam which he put out and we sold maybe 10 or 12, one of those kind of deals, but from all that Sam and I became good friends.

The job I had I was through work probably 2 or 3 o'clock in the afternoon and I'd drive by the studio and if he wasn't tied up working well we'd go next door to Miss Taylor's restaurant and drink coffee and just chit chat about the business and "What do you think?" and "What do you think we need to do?" just in general and one day we were having coffee and his secretary was there, Miss Marion Keisker was with us and she asked Sam "Did you ever talk to that boy that was in here about a year ago that cut that demo for his mother's .." she gave the details and he said "No." So I'd say about probably a week or two went by and every day that went by and I saw him and be there having coffee together I'd always ask him "Oh by the way did you ever contact that boy?" cos I kept that in my mind.

So finally one day Marion again was having coffee with us and he turned to her and asked her and... I said "I haven't even heard this guy's name yet, even", and he turned to Marion and says "Get that guy, have you still got his telephone number?" She says "Yeah" and he said "Give it to Scotty" and he turned to me and said "You call him and ask him to come over to your house and see what you think." And that was fine. So in a little

bit Marion goes and comes back and gives me the piece of paper with his number on it and I looked at it and I say "His name – Elvis Presley – what kind of a name is that?" And that was really all that was said and goodbye.

When I got home that afternoon I called and his mother answered and she said that he was at the theatre I believe and that she'd have him call when he got back. So a couple of hours later he called and I told him that I was working with Sam Phillips and he was looking for material, looking for artists blah, blah and would he be interested in doing an audition and he said "Well sure." And I asked him to come over to my house, which was on Bill's Avenue, the next day which was July the, Sunday would have been the 4th, no 3rd, no 4th cos Memphis didn't shoot fireworks on Sunday but Sunday they did actually celebrate it on next day on Monday, that's the way it went. He came over that Sunday and he sat around and he played and sang everything, it seemed like he knew every song in the world and, but he didn't know how to play half of them. But he'd play along and when he didn't know the chords he'd just keep playing, keep singing. And this went on for a couple of hours.

Bill Black at that time, he lived just a few doors down the street from me and he came down to sit in, just listening with us for a little while and left. Then when Elvis left I told Elvis I said "Either I or Sam will probably be calling you about coming into the studio". I called Sam and I told him I said "Well it seems like the boy knows all the songs. Being as young as he is he's got a good voice", and Sam said "Well I'll call him and ask him to come in tomorrow night", which would have been Monday night and said "Can you and Bill come in and do a little background? I don't want the whole band, I just need a little noise behind him to see what he sounds like". And we said "Sure." Bill came back down and I asked Bill, I said "Bill what did you think of him?" And he said "Alright - seems like a new bunch of songs, he sounds pretty good you know? Had good timing", and so forth, that kind of thing. And so we went down to the studio the next night, Monday night and there again, he went through all these different songs, just whatever came to mind, Sam didn't request anything or anything.

It was at least 10 o'clock, it was getting late, we were about ready to go to the house cos it was still just an audition. And Elvis stood up and started playing his guitar and singing That's Alright and Bill started slapping his bass and playing along with him. I had never heard the song, Bill had never heard it and I took the guitar and started playing, looking for something, we were just jamming. The door to the control room was open and Sam stuck his head out and said "What are you guys doing?" We said "we're just goofing around" and he said "Well just do it a little more". Cos the mikes weren't on or anything and he said "Let me go and turn the mikes on" or whatever and we got on the mike, went through it 2 or 3 times and that was it. Lord am I glad or am I sorry, I don't know!

Q So tell me a bit about The Blue Moon Boys and your fellow musicians Bill and DJ.
Well Blue Moon Boys was just Bill and myself. They dropped that name when we left Sun. DJ never recorded with us. We started using DJ when we went to the Louisiana Hayride and he did a lot of shows with us during the period we were on Sun. Heartbreak Hotel was the first thing he played on when we came to Nashville to RCA.

Q Did all this phenomenon with rock and roll happen overnight or did it slowly happen?
Well, actually the first thing is – what is rock and roll? Alan Freed had a disc jockey show up in, where was he? He was the one that coined that phrase. I suppose everybody knows really what the term really means – it came from black music and they

would use that term to get across their message. I don't know, that name did stick when he started calling it rock and roll. Before that Elvis was being called the Hillbilly Cat, Rockabilly – gosh I don't know what else they called him. I'm sure he had some good names. But for us, as far as the band, we just enjoyed playing – there wasn't a producer, there wasn't somebody who said you gotta play something this way or that way – they let us do what we wanted to do.

Q What happened after that? Did you start working with Elvis full time? When did you also become his manager?
Well the first thing, the group I was telling you about that I had, The Starlite Wranglers, we were doing a Friday and Saturday gig at a small club here in town, Bel Air Club, and that was the first thing after we cut That's Alright – then a few days went by and we finally came up with the B-side and that came up in really the same way, cos we went back in a couple of days later and Elvis started going through all different songs. Sam would think of something or I would think of something and he'd try it "Do you know so and so?" "Yeah I know it" – and he'd try something else just to. Bill was sitting on his bass fiddle, I don't know, if you have a bass just laying on the floor and he was sitting, just sitting on it and he started beating on it and singing Blue Moon of Kentucky which was a waltz country song by Bill Monroe and he was singing it in falsetto, high tenor you know, up tempo and Elvis knew the song and he started singing along with him. That was the B-side, it was that simple.

Q When you were in the studio, how many takes would it take to do songs?
Well, once we landed on something that he knew and liked, it might have been something that Sam had put out before or whatever – but when he liked the song and everything, well it didn't take us too long. He might miss a word, I might miss a

chord, Sam would goof sometimes when we were recording, but we're talking about skin of your teeth back in those days, but once we'd got everything in order, it didn't take too many takes. It was just mainly – when he was satisfied that he'd done his best singing, it was the main thing.

Q **Was he a perfectionist?**
It was the feel, he wanted to feel, we all felt the same way, if I might have missed a note or not hit a note perfect, if the total thing felt good, that's what counted. I mean I might have played something fantastic and I would never have played the same thing twice anyway but when I played if it felt good, it was the same thing. Elvis was the same way.

Q **Can you tell us a bit about where we are now?**
Well, we're in RCAB in Nashville. We cut a few things here. Course I guess most of our recording was done in California and some of the hits were done, a few were done in New York too. But all the time I was with him, we did several of them here.

Q **Tell us about how you became his manager and what that relationship was like.**
Well after we put out that first record, of course the local DJs around Memphis started getting calls and everything. A couple of other people that were "music managers" and what have you and everybody was calling him. The three of us – Bill, Sam, myself and Elvis - were all just sitting chatting one day and he was talking about the people calling him and he said "Well I don't know what to tell them". And it was actually Sam's idea he said "Well I'll tell you what. Scotty, why don't you sign up as manager for a year and it'll give us time to look for somebody that we all trust and want to work with." And that's the way it happened and of course, we had Bob Neil came in, who was a local disc jockey and he started booking us

in and around Memphis, Arkansas, Mississippi, locally – cos he was on a radio station, I think he was on about 6 o'clock in the morning and at that time in the morning the station really went out.

Q What was life on the road like?
Starting off like that, none of us had ever been on the road so number one you'd have an experience and then pretty soon you'd start to get tired and say will this never end. And yet tomorrow the next show will be better, there'll be a better show, there'll be more money, it'll be, you know, everything is supposed to go up. But we were just typical, like, I won't say like any other band that's out there but – we'd have our fusses and everything. Bill and I did most of the driving in the early days then when DJ joined us, he did some of the driving too.

We had a problem with Elvis when he was driving – he was a good driver, a very good driver – but for some reason he just could not read road signs. If you came to a fork in the road, well, he'd take the wrong one every time. But he was a good driver. DJ was a good driver. We were on the road when they were just starting to build interstates and we left Memphis going – I don't know where we were going – but, we got to St Louis where they had just built the brand new ring road around, and it was around 11 o'clock at night or something like that. I had been driving and I turned it over to DJ and got over in the other seat and went to sleep. Bill and Elvis were in the back seat. I woke up in daylight, sitting on the side of the road, still asleep and I said "Where are we at?" and he says "Still in St Louis." He said "I can't get off this damn road." We never let him forget it either. He'll probably bring it up.

Q What was the music scene like when you went to the live events?
In the very, very, very early days when Bob Naylor was

booking us, we were doing a lot of little country schoolhouses, I say country schoolhouses cos they were little towns and the schoolhouses would be outside of the city limits maybe. And say the show was starting at 7 o'clock we would get there at 7.30 and there wouldn't be a soul anywhere. And you had to take your own PAs – I mean they had PAs in those little places like that, it was just had a microphone that sometimes just plugged into my little amplifier. There wasn't even any equipment there – you'd take all of that. We were the whole show and we started getting some other people to go with us. Arnie Wheeler was a country artist back then – he went with us on a lot. But anyway, we would get there about 7.30, and get set up, 8 o'clock doors open and just whoof! every body was there. Well, they'd heard the record on the radio but they hadn't seen him. And they were just sitting.

Well Bill started cutting up cos the bass player back in those days, especially on country acts, the bass player always had to dress up in, be a clown but he started whooping and hollering, sitting on the bass, riding the bass and just cutting up you know. And the people would start coming alive by watching him and then they would get into the music and that's what really got him started. I mean he, and everything he'd do, they'd clap and carry on and he'd embellish on it.

Q And had he always had those dance moves and the lip snarl or did that come later?
The only thing that he had natural that I know of was the first thing we did at the Overton Park Shell that was the first actual stage performance in front of an audience and Bob Naylor got us on that as a closing, actually as an extra act – Slim Whitman was the featured singer on that. And for me the guitar player, if he's standing up, usually will either pat his foot, keep in time or sit down and if he doesn't do it he doesn't do anything. But Elvis, when he was singing and playing he'd always raise up

on the balls of his feet, both feet. And with the big breeches legs back then, they started flapping and he looked like he was really getting going with it. And that was what they were really laughing about, going on about.

Q Is there any myths you want to dispel about anything that's out there in the media?
If you could name them, I could tell you a whole bunch of them but they just don't come right to mind.

Q I had June 27th – was that another meeting?
July 4th was the first day I met him – I talked to him on the phone the day before. Of course I found out much later that he had been in Sun before and had done some of those little demos supposedly for his mother. But he had never mentioned that.

Q So when was the turning point where Sun and RCA came in there? When did that change? There was '54/'55 were the Sun sessions, we discussed those. When did you guys go from Sun to RCA?
Well, there had been several people trying to buy us contracts and Parker came into the deal and set the whole thing up with RCA and they paid Sam the money. And this was when we went to RCA and cut the first record.

Q And can you tell us a bit about that?
Well, it was just another studio date we did it at Trafco. Their building was down on McGavock Street and in the lower floor RCA had rented the studio and that's where we cut Heartbreak Hotel.

Q Tell me, what were your feelings about Colonel Parker and that change in management? What did you make of that?
Well, I probably don't want to get into that.

Q OK, tell me about the movies. I heard you were in a couple of the movies. What did you make of the soundtracks?

We did a couple of the early ones with him as extras. Well it was actually the band in one, the first one – I always say the first one, we weren't in – that was interesting. We went out to – when he did Love Me Tender – they took The Jordanaires, Bill, DJ, myself and Elvis they had us all come out to a bungalow on the lot at MGM and it was all pre set-up, we knew that later, cos Elvis didn't know anything either about it. You've seen the movie, you know what it was about. So we go into our regular show we're doing on the tour. And they said "No that's not the kind of music we want, sorry." "That was ok thank you very much". Then we see the movie and we've been playing hillbilly music all our lives. But it was set up – Ken Derby, who was the musical director, he had his own guys he wanted to use. I understand those kind of things. It wasn't bad, you just knew it was pre-done.

Q What did you make of Elvis as an actor?

I just wish he could have got some real scripts later on. When they found out they could make some money off of him, I guess, well, he went ahead and did it – I never will understand why. He just wouldn't put his foot down on management and say "I will not do this. Give me something." He did have a chance at A Star is Born – they had that in mind for him, and then Parker wouldn't let him do it.

Q What did you think of Elvis as a person?

Well, he was just a regular guy. With all the stuff that hit him at such an early age and so fast - he never really had a chance to grow up. He always had his so-called friends around him and he just never grew up.

Q Cos I was going to ask you about the money, it's fascinating, but if you don't want to talk about it.
That happened here by the way. Yes, he cut that song here in …… yeah, I think Jerry Reed wrote and played on.

Q Do you think that early on drugs were affecting Elvis in the early years?
It didn't affect his music really at the time that I was with him. He didn't really get into that, that started when he was in the army, he started taking binnies. I think they used to give them when they were going out on manoeuvres because he was driving a tank. It used to keep you awake and that was the normal thing. But I guess he got to liking them pretty good and then went onto different stuff. I don't know really all the background on that just what I read.

Q What did you think of The Jordanaires and what did they bring to the Elvis sound?
What can you say, when he found a group he liked and he liked The Jordanaires from even before he'd ever recorded with them so it was just natural that they would work with him. They still sound good, you know.

Q Where do you think Elvis got a lot of his influence?
Mostly from religion music. He loved quartets, he loved The Jordanaires, The Blackwood Brothers, just the way he was raised, he used to go to all night singings and such. I guess that's where he first met The Jordanaires maybe – he met them in Memphis - they were there on a show I think.

Q What about your guitars, what did you use back then?
On the first record I had an ES-295, Gibson ES-295. And when I first came out of the navy I bought a Fender and, mainly because in the navy there were a couple of other guys on there who played a little bit, and we'd bought Japanese guitars when

going to port and the frets were made out of beer cans cos you'd wear the frets out in 30 days. But we were always sitting down so they were thin guitars, like Fenders, call them copies of Fenders. And when I came out I bought a Fender but then standing up I couldn't keep it still, it kept getting away from me. And I was walking down town one day by the music store and they had just put one of the ES-295s in there which was gold coloured and all the hardware was gold-plated and everything and I said "I gotta have it." And I went in and made a trade and got that, and that's what I had when we first got started. I kept it through the first 4 records.

On the 5th record I got an EchoSonic amplifier which had an echo in it that, I'd heard this on one record by Chet Atkins and my thought was that if I had that – cos I was always worried we'd do something and when Sam was using the slapback echo on the whole song, that when we went out to do the show it would sound lah, you know, it didn't have the pep then. And I knew that if I could get that amplifier then at least one instrument would have the right sound. And I called Nashville and I don't remember who I talked to now but I found out somehow or another from chat that Ray Butts was in Cairo, Illinois, a music store that had designed this amp and I drove up there to see him and he said "Yeah, be glad to build you one." Now this is 1954 and it only cost $500 for that amplifier. I still have it.

Q Shake, Rattle and Roll – was this the world's first glimpse of Elvis?
Yeah, probably so. They might have heard the name. Yeah.

Q Hound Dog – can you describe what made the early Elvis sound unique in musical terms?
There again, we just did what we felt. We only had 3 Jordanaires on that. Gordon Stoker was playing piano cos Shorty Long had another gig he had to go to he was working on a stage show and

so he had to leave. And Gordon took over piano and so we just had the 3 Jordanaires singing on that. And you can tell it if you listen to it real close with a musical ear. I'm trying to be real nice about Tez. But let me interject this, when everything got that it felt good for everybody, that was the cut.

Q Do you think the early television performances were good in musical terms?
No, because they could have been so much better, you weren't allowed to, you couldn't set a mike in front, you couldn't dare see a microphone then or anything, the mike was probably way up in the air. You know how television used to be. Now they finally got away from that – ok, you're playing the guitar or what, let me see it.

Q They used to put the drummer behind the curtain?
Yeah, oh yeah. DJ used to play at the Hayride, that's when we first met him – he was playing behind a screen. There was a shadow, you could see the shadow but you didn't see him. Now you don't wanna see him!

Q Do you think the guitar breaks were important in the early arrangements?
Well, I don't know if they would have been important or not. They were just of the style of the day, as it has always been. A singer will sing a verse or two, then whether it's the guitar or a piano or whatever it is then the instrumental pad goes in there too. Better leave that up to the beholding of the people listening I guess.

Q Was there anything out of the ordinary in Elvis' version of Blue Suede Shoes and Tutti Frutti that was better than the original renditions?
Just that we did them probably faster maybe. Again we just did it the way we felt it. RCA, Steve Scholes whatever had been

trying to get, when Carl's record was doing real good, they'd been trying to get Elvis to cover it and Elvis wouldn't do it. He said "No, I'm not going to cover it, cos Carl's a friend of mine, we work the shows together", and so forth. We were going to New York, I can't remember which show we were going to be on. But Carl had one also up there and they'd had, that's when Carl had the wreck and Bill, DJ and myself were on our way up to there and we were.

We went by to see Carl in the hospital and they all said send him a telegram or call in with something also. But he was already in New York. And when we got to New York he said he wanted to do Blue Suede Shoes on the show. He was doing it for Carl, you know, he wasn't trying to take away anything. Cos they had been pushing him trying to get him to do it before Carl had the wreck.

Q Do you think Heartbreak Hotel was the first real Elvis classic?
Well, yeah cos it was the first record on RCA and of course it had been the first one that was played all over the whole country. Before that it was strictly a southern regional hit kind of thing.

Q And Suspicious Minds – was this the perfect repertoire for Elvis? Did it sum up what was happening in his life at the time?
No, I never thought of it that way. I don't know. Could be.

Q American Trilogy – the ultimate Elvis song?
See that was done originally by Micky Newberry. Elvis had heard it. I think he believed it was just a good show tune to do on stage and maybe make some people stand up straighter and salute or so – political type thing you know.

Q Do you think he was a perfectionist in terms of his performances, Elvis?

Well a perfectionist you never knew what he was going to do. I mean when he went on stage you didn't know what he was going to do. There was perfection maybe in his own way and how he was going to do something but we didn't know what he was going to do.

Q Could the effect of Elvis' decline in health be seen in his later performances do you think?

Well, the only time I saw him was when he was on video or something. The last time I saw him, I can't remember what the show was, where he had gained so much weight and I could tell there was something wrong but I didn't know what.

Q Can you remember where you were when he passed away and what your feelings were?

Yeah, I was in the control room at Monument Studios doing some editing as such.

Q And how did you feel?

I don't know, well I guess just saddened of course.

Q Do you think Elvis is overrated or do you think he's the king?

He wouldn't have liked the title king, I know that for sure. If we could break everything down, he would be underrated in some things and he'd be overrated in other things. So I'd just leave that to the individual.

Q What about the book? Can you mention anything about the book and how that came about?

Jim Dickerson was the one that did the book on me. He'd just been pestering me to do it and I finally gave in – that's all I know.

Q Did your daughter have something to do with that?
Yeah, our daughter was friends of his and that came about in a roundabout way, Vicky.

Q Is there anything you might like to add?
No I'm fine if you've got enough. The book had been out of print for some time but they've done another printing and brought it up to date, added another chapter about all my illnesses and hospital stays and such mostly.

Q Are you ok now?
Yeah, I got a couple of nice holes in my head. I guess so.

Q Do you pick up the guitar now?
Yeah, I still try to play a little bit. I'm still having trouble with my right arm and hand but part of that's just pure age, arthritis.

Q And if I were to say that your guitar playing was a major role in the history of American popular music, what would you say?
Thank you!

ABOUT CODA BOOKS

Most Coda books are edited and endorsed by Emmy Award winning filmmaker and concert promoter Bob Carruthers. Over the last 20 years Bob has filmed and promoted tours, concerts and made documentaries all over Britain and Europe in venues ranging from Hammersmith Odeon to Murrayfield Stadium, with artists such as Bryan Adams, Spandau Ballet, Jethro Tull, Status Quo and Katherine Jenkins.

The 'Uncensored On the Record' series explores the careers of many of music's greatest legends, encompassing a wide range of genres including classic rock, pop, heavy metal, punk, country, classical and soul.

For more information visit **www.codabooks.com**.

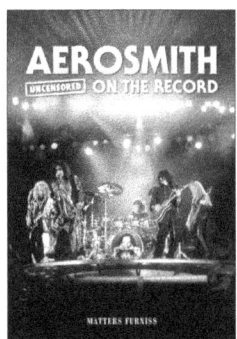
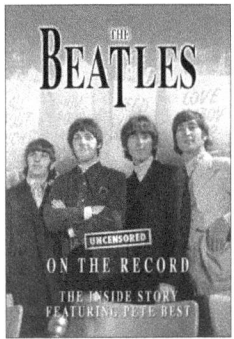

www.ingramcontent.com/pod-product-compliance
Lightning Source LLC
LaVergne TN
LVHW090116080426
835507LV00040B/914